CABLE TV

CABLE TV
Regulation or Competition?

Robert W. Crandall
and
Harold Furchtgott-Roth

THE BROOKINGS INSTITUTION
Washington, D.C.

Library of Congress Cataloging-in-Publication Data

Crandall, Robert W.
    Cable TV : regulation or competition? / Robert W. Crandall, Harold Furchtgott-Roth.
    p. cm.
    Includes index.
    ISBN 0-8157-1610-9 (cloth : alk. paper). — ISBN 0-8157-1609-5 (pbk. : alk.
paper) 1. Cable television—Deregulation—United States. 2. Cable television—
United States. 3. Cable television—Law and legislation—United
States. 4. Competition—United States. I. Furchtgott-Roth, Harold W. II. Title.
HE8700.72.U6C73   1996
384.55'51—dc20   95-51319
                                                                                          CIP

9 8 7 6 5 4 3 2 1

The paper used in this publication meets the minimum
requirements of the American National Standard for Information Sciences—
Permanence of Paper for Printed
Library Materials, ANSI Z39.48-1984

Typeset in Sabon

Composition by Automated Graphic Systems
White Plains, Maryland

Printed by R. R. Donnelley and Sons, Co.
Harrisonburg, Virginia

THE BROOKINGS INSTITUTION

The Brookings Institution is an independent organization devoted to nonpartisan research, education, and publication in economics, government, foreign policy, and the social sciences generally. Its principal purposes are to aid in the development of sound public policies and to promote public understanding of issues of national importance.

The Institution was founded on December 8, 1927, to merge the activities of the Institute for Government Research, founded in 1916, the Institute of Economics, founded in 1922, and the Robert Brookings Graduate School of Economics and Government, founded in 1924.

The Board of Trustees is responsible for the general administration of the Institution, while the immediate direction of the policies, program, and staff is vested in the President, assisted by an advisory committee of the officers and staff. The by-laws of the Institution state: "It is the function of the Trustees to make possible the conduct of scientific research, and publication, under the most favorable conditions, and to safeguard the independence of the research staff in the pursuit of their studies and in the publication of the results of such studies. It is not a part of their function to determine, control, or influence the conduct of particular investigations or the conclusions reached."

The President bears final responsibility for the decision to publish a manuscript as a Brookings book. In reaching his judgment on the competence, accuracy, and objectivity of each study, the President is advised by the director of the appropriate research program and weighs the views of a panel of expert outside readers who report to him in confidence on the quality of the work. Publication of a work signifies that it is deemed a competent treatment worthy of public consideration but does not imply endorsement of conclusions or recommendations.

The Institution maintains its position of neutrality on issues of public policy in order to safeguard the intellectual freedom of the staff. Hence interpretations or conclusions in Brookings publications should be understood to be solely those of the authors and should not be attributed to the Institution, to its trustees, officers, or other staff members, or to the organizations that support its research.

Foreword

THE CABLE television industry is only one source of video programming for U.S. households, but it is clearly the most important. Traditional broadcast stations, video cassettes, wireless cable, and direct broadcast satellites compete with it for viewers, but nearly two-thirds of all households subscribe to a local cable service. Because few households have access to more than one service, however, Congress has frequently expressed concern that local cable operators may be charging inflated monopoly rates. As a result, in 1992 it passed legislation over President Bush's veto that established wide federal regulation of cable television for the first time, a surprising action considering the tendency to embrace economic deregulation in the 1970s and 1980s.

The 1992 act was even more surprising because Congress had passed a law in 1986 that had ended state and local regulation for all but a few cable systems. Now in 1996 it has reversed itself once again with the Telecommunications Act, which removes most cable television services from formal rate regulation, although most of the 1992 act's regulatory provisions remain.

In this book Robert Crandall of the Economic Studies program at Brookings and Harold Furchtgott-Roth of the House Energy and Commerce Committee show that the 1984 deregulation was followed by an extraordinary expansion of cable services. Even if cable operators enjoyed some monopoly power and increased rates between 1986 and 1992, they provided subscribers with many more and better-quality viewing choices. The reimposition of rate regulation in 1992 sharply reduced cash flows in the cable industry and, if the 1996 act had not been passed, may have compromised the incentives to further improve service quality.

The authors examine the prospects of the newer multichannel video technologies and conclude that in the next few years the market is likely to become contestable through the development of direct broadcast satellites, telephone company broadband networks, and cellular cable. They also conclude that the risks of deregulating cable are likely to be small, especially compared with the costs of trying to control the rates of such a differentiated service.

The authors are grateful for helpful criticisms and suggestions from Michael Baumann, Charles Jackson, Bruce Owen, Jeffrey Smith, and Clifford Winston. Research assistance was provided by Jeffrey McConnell, Jeffrey Santos, and Stephanie Wilshusen. James Schneider edited the manuscript, Cynthia Iglesias verified its factual content, Trish Weisman proofread it, and Mary Mortenson compiled the index.

This study was funded in part by the Alex C. Walker Educational and Charitable Foundation.

The views expressed in this book are those of the authors and should not be ascribed to the trustees, officers, or other staff members of the Brookings Institution.

MICHAEL H. ARMACOST
President

March 1996
Washington, D.C.

Contents

ix

Tables

Figures

CHAPTER ONE

The Evolution of Cable Television

ALTHOUGH cable television began on a very small scale less than half a century ago as a complement to regulated television broadcasting, it has evolved into a major force in an increasingly dynamic U.S. telecommunications-information-entertainment sector. It not only reaches nearly two-thirds of all U.S. households and passes all but 5 percent of the country's homes, but it offers one of the three wires into these homes (the other two, of course, are connected to the local telephone company and the electric utility). The local cable operator thus has a promising means for developing the information superhighway of the future. But that development faces some serious obstacles. The rapid evolution of cable television was unanticipated by federal regulators and Congress. Their attempts to monitor the industry and ensure it operates for the benefit of the public have resolved themselves into alternating periods of benign neglect and strict regulation. These actions, their effects on the industry, and policies that can facilitate competition and provide greater benefits for consumers are the subjects of this book.

The Early History

Cable television began as shared noncommercial community antenna television services to improve signal reception in areas where it was poor. An antenna could be installed on a hilltop and broadcast signals received and retransmitted through a cable that fed the households in valleys and other areas of restricted reception. Historians place the first such system either in Mahoney City, Pennsylvania, in 1948 or Astoria, Oregon, in 1949. The first subscription cable system was established in Lansford, Pennsylvania, in 1950.[1]

These early systems were very limited. They could carry only a few channels, reflecting both the state of transmission technology and the scarcity of

1. See Stanley M. Besen and Robert W. Crandall, "The Deregulation of Cable Television," *Law and Contemporary Problems,* vol. 44 (Winter 1981), pp. 77–124.

nearby channels to retransmit, and their customers were few. The Federal Communications Commission's spectrum-allocation decisions in the 1950s scattered the twelve VHF television frequencies across the country so as to provide at least two or three VHF signals to major metropolitan areas. There were more UHF allocations, but broadcasters were slow to develop them because most television sets could not receive UHF signals or could not tune them in very well. And there were no alternatives. Non-broadcast programming was not offered: audiences accessible through cable were too small and the cost of distribution too high.[2] The idea of special programming offered for a fee in addition to the basic subscription cost had not yet been developed; indeed, even by the 1960s, premium programming was offered experimentally to just a few homes.[3] The result was slow growth for the industry; it took fifteen years, 1948–63, to connect the first million subscribers.[4]

As late as 1959 the Federal Communications Commission considered cable television simply a local retransmission service; it seemed to pose no threat of competition to broadcast television, which the commission carefully regulated.[5] But as the cable industry began to grow more rapidly as a result of retransmitting distant broadcast signals through the use of microwave circuitry or very tall antennas, the FCC was forced to address the possibility that cable operations might upset the agency's television allocations plan, which was meant to encourage localism and required broadcasters with monopoly franchises to subsidize uneconomical local programming. In 1962 the commission acted to limit cable's encroachment on local broadcasters' monopolies by requiring a microwave carrier to demonstrate that it would carry local signals and not distant ones that duplicated the programming of the local stations.[6]

As cable's growth accelerated in the next few years, fear of the technology permeated the FCC to such an extent that in 1966 it announced broad restrictions on the medium. No system in the largest one hundred markets would be able to import a distant signal unless it could show that such

2. Until satellite delivery was developed in the late 1970s, programs had to be distributed by expensive microwave circuits or the physical delivery of film or tape. The microwave facilities could be leased at very high rates from telephone companies or they could be constructed for the sole use of cable systems.

3. Roger G. Noll, Merton J. Peck, and John J. McGowan, *Economic Aspects of Television Regulation* (Brookings, 1973), chap. 5.

4. Besen and Crandall, "Deregulation of Cable Television," p. 80.

5. 26 FCC 403 (1959).

6. 32 FCC 459 (1962).

action was in the public interest, which was defined to include the growth of UHF television service.[7] Because the FCC was predisposed to accept the argument that the expansion of multichannel cable systems would reduce the profitability of prospective UHF stations, few systems bothered to apply for permission to import distant signals into the larger television markets. The commission even asked Congress to forbid cable systems from originating programming, but this legislation was never passed.[8]

Some observers contend that this high-water mark of repressive regulation reflected the FCC's desire to have Congress resolve the issues involving copyright and retransmission consent. Should cable systems be required to negotiate with stations or the owners of the copyrighted programming carried by the stations before retransmitting their signals? During the next two and one-half decades, Congress would change course several times on copyright fees and retransmission consent, but the matter remains a major unresolved issue in cable regulation.[9]

In 1972 the FCC announced sweeping new rules governing cable television operations. A cable system had to carry all local broadcast signals. Depending on the size of the local market, systems would be permitted to import signals from up to three networks and up to three independent stations to fill out service. In offering imported signals, cable operators could not leapfrog nearby stations in favor of large-market independent stations. Syndicated programming on local stations was to be protected from competition of identical programming on imported signals by blacking out those signals. Systems with 3,500 subscribers or more had to originate some of their own programming. Channels were to be set aside for government, education, and public access. Operators had to expand capacity if all channels were in use for more than a specified percentage of the week. Finally, premium programming, with its extra cost to viewers, was virtually banned by a bizarre ruling limiting such programming to one feature film more than two years old and less than ten years old per week for one week of each month. The same ruling effectively prohibited all premium exhibition of live sporting events that had been traditionally available on "free" broadcast television.[10]

7. 2 FCC 2d 725 (1966).
8. Besen and Crandall, "Deregulation of Cable Television," pp. 90–91.
9. The Cable Television Consumer Protection and Competition Act of 1992 requires cable systems to negotiate retransmission consent with broadcast stations whose signals they carry. It also requires that cable systems carry all local stations in their market if the stations demand carriage, a requirement that has been the subject of considerable litigation.
10. The details of this extraordinary ruling may be found in the rules published with the Federal Communications Commission, *Cable Television Report and Order and Recon-*

These incredible rules, the result of a compromise between broadcast and cable interests, were defended by the FCC as being in the public interest because they protected local broadcasting while allowing some growth for cable. Their life was short, however; the commission began to reconsider the rules as early as 1974, and the most extreme provisions were softened or repealed. At first the FCC altered or dropped the less consequential restrictions, such as the limitation on importing distant signals even when local stations were not broadcasting. The reconsideration accelerated when the commission abandoned the leapfrogging restrictions; it had come to believe that they were too burdensome and that the danger of encouraging the development of national superstations, with their threat of stifling local stations, had been overstated.

In fact, superstations did materialize after the leapfrogging rules were repealed, in part because of a change in commission policy on receive-only satellite dishes. Before 1977, cable systems had been required to use 9-meter satellite dishes to guarantee signal quality. However, the commission was forced to admit that cable owners did not need the assistance of regulators to decide whether the expense of a 9-meter dish was justified by improved signal quality. It authorized cable systems to use 4.5-meter dishes if they wished, lowering the cost of importing distant signals.[11] Superstations such as WTBS (Atlanta), WGN (Chicago), and WOR (New York) that programmed for a national cable audience were soon available through the smaller dishes.

The deregulatory process accelerated in 1977. The courts vacated the rules restricting premium channels, and the FCC would not consider rewriting the rules.[12] About the same time, the commission launched an inquiry into the economics of the cable industry that would result in the abandonment by 1979 of most of the restrictions on how many and what kind of signals cable companies could carry. As the 1980s dawned, therefore, cable was free of the most repressive federal regulatory provisions that had limited its ability to offer diverse programming, but it was still subject to regulation by municipal or state franchising or regulatory authorities.

From Community Access Television to Cablecasting

In the early 1970s, when cable television was still considered primarily a medium for retransmitting broadcast signals, the success of a franchise was

---

sideration, February 3, 1972. (CFR, Title 47, chap. 1, pt. 76, D, F, and G.)
  11. 62 FCC 2d 901 (1977).
  12. *Home Box Office v. FCC,* 567 F.2d 9 (1977), *cert. denied,* 434 U.S. 829 (1977).

Table 1-1. *Cable Television Systems and Subscribers as of January 1, Selected Years, 1960–95*

Year	Number of systems	Subscribers (millions)	Year	Number of systems	Subscribers (millions)
1960	640	0.65	1983	5,600	25.00
1962	800	0.85	1984	6,200	29.00
1964	1,200	1.09	1985	6,600	32.00
1966	1,570	1.58	1986	7,500	37.50
1968	2,000	2.80	1987	7,900	41.00
1970	2,490	4.50	1988	8,500	44.00
1972	2,841	6.00	1989	9,050	47.50
1974	3,158	8.70	1990	9,575	50.00
1976	3,681	10.80	1991	10,704	51.00
1978	3,875	13.00	1992	11,035	53.00
1980	4,225	16.00	1993	11,108	54.20
1981	4,375	18.30	1994	11,214	55.30
1982	4,825	21.00	1995	11,351	56.50

Source: Warren Publishing, *Television and Cable Factbook, 1995* (Washington, 1995), p. F-2.

tied to importing signals from Chicago or New York or Los Angeles into television-starved communities in central Illinois or New Jersey or California. Few expected motion picture companies to embrace television as a medium for distributing their products; indeed, most studios thought of television as the enemy until well into the 1970s. Cable origination of live sporting events might have been a possibility, but the FCC had banned these live broadcasts as part of its grand 1972 broadcaster–cable industry compromise. Even retransmission was limited by a commission still intent on protecting the broadcasting industry.[13] The FCC restrictions were mildly successful; cable subscriber growth slowed somewhat in the 1970s (table 1-1).

Once the courts disallowed the commission's restrictions on premium channels, however, cable television entered a new era. Equally important to the new freedom, low-cost satellite transmission was replacing terrestrial microwave networks as the principal means of distributing programming to both cable systems and broadcast stations. Assembling a terrestrial network of microwave circuits to connect thousands of system distribution

13. The FCC considered retransmission a threat for two reasons. First, the availability of additional programs would fragment the audience and complicate advertisers' purchasing strategies. Second, retransmission might disrupt program suppliers' practice of granting exclusive licenses for the use of programs for a stated time because, as long as the cable companies were not required to pay copyright fees, suppliers could not prevent cable owners from importing licensed programs via distant signals.

points (known as headends) had been an expensive barrier to market entry for cablecasting. With satellite technology the path was clear for cable operators to expand. By the early 1980s Nickelodeon, Black Entertainment Television, and other attractive new networks were available through satellite delivery for inclusion with the systems' basic service package. Cable finally had something more than broadcast network programming and tired reruns or local programming from independent stations to offer subscribers.

Home Box Office began cable's premium-channel revolution in 1972, but it did not initiate satellite delivery until 1975. After a 1977 court decision allowed HBO to use satellite delivery freely, Showtime, the second premium movie service, initiated satellite delivery.[14] By 1979 there were ten premium networks, available individually or in groups for a separate monthly charge, although most of them were small and would not survive. Eleven basic cable networks, including Nickelodeon, were available to round out systems' channel offerings. Further growth was impeded by the limited capacity of the cable systems themselves. Seventy-seven percent of all systems offered twelve channels or fewer in 1976, and 88 percent offered twenty or fewer.[15] By limiting programming choices, FCC regulation had made developing the capacity to offer more channels uneconomical.

As deregulation took hold, more programming became available, and the electronic equipment used in distribution systems improved, cable systems rapidly expanded their capacity. Forty-three percent of systems (serving 68 percent of the country's subscribers) offered twenty or more channels by 1983. Sixty-five percent of all systems (serving 90 percent of subscribers) offered that many by 1987. By the end of 1989 the average subscriber had a choice of thirty-one channels.[16] There were more than fifty basic cable networks available by satellite and about ten premium channels as well as a number of regional sports networks. In just ten years, the number of channels had more than trebled and the average number of channels available more than doubled.[17]

14. *Home Box Office v. FCC,* 567 F.2d 9 (1977), *cert. denied,* 434 U.S. 829 (1977).

15. National Telecommunications and Information Administration, *Video Program Distribution and Cable Television: Current Policy Issues and Recommendations* (June 1988), p. 10.

16. General Accounting Office, *Follow-Up National Survey of Cable Television Rates and Services,* GAO/RCED 90-199 (June 1990).

17. Much of this growth in average capacity reflected the growth of new large-market systems that had been built after the FCC had rescinded some 1972 rules or they were overturned by the courts. Before 1977 few of these systems would have been viable because

This rapid growth in service was induced in part by the deregulatory spirit of the 1980s. After 1977 the FCC had all but abandoned its attempts to control cable television programming. But cable had developed as a municipally franchised service that was also subject to local government franchise fees, municipal or state regulation of rates, and various local service requirements such as free cable for schools and town halls. As cable grew into a service providing national network programming delivered by satellite, pressure from the Reagan administration and the cable industry began to build to eliminate municipal service requirements and regulation of rates. Congress responded by passing the Cable Communications Policy Act of 1984, requiring that the rates of all cable systems facing "effective competition" from regular broadcasting sources (known as off-air broadcasting), as determined by the FCC, be deregulated. But the act required that municipal franchising continue, with fees limited to 5 percent of revenues from subscribers. The result was nearly full rate deregulation from mid-1986 until early 1993.[18] In the same legislation, however, Congress moved to block one promising avenue of competition for cable television by denying telephone companies the right to offer cable service in their telephone franchise areas.[19]

The FCC established the benchmark for effective competition as the presence of three or more off-air broadcast signals that were viewed by significant numbers of people or that transmitted an acceptable signal in the local cable franchise area.[20] In effect, the ruling barred rate regulation for all but a few cable systems.[21] Rate deregulation encouraged improved service quality and expanded channel capacity, but it also allowed cable operators to raise rates at their own discretion, and many exercised this

---

the FCC's rules prevented them from offering anything of much value to potential subscribers.

18. This is not to say that rates were tightly regulated before the effective date of deregulation. Most municipalities provided at best casual supervision of subscriber rates for basic cable services. Premium services were never regulated by municipal or state authorities. See chapters 2 and 3.

19. There is an economic rationale for limiting telephone company investments in cable television: legislators fear that these companies might attempt to subsidize the investments with funds from their regulated telephone monopoly services. There are, however, other safeguards besides outright prohibition of their involvement in cable activities, including structurally separate facilities and the substitution of price caps for cost-based regulation of telephone services.

20. 50 FR 18637 (1985).

21. The National League of Cities reported to the FCC that cable had been deregulated in more than 99 percent of its member cities. Comments filed in MM docket no. 84-1296 (December 4, 1987), as reported in 5 FCC Rcd 362 (1990).

discretion repeatedly until Congress moved to reimpose rate regulation in the 1992 Cable Television Consumer Protection and Competition Act.[22]

A study by the General Accounting Office that supplied much of the impetus for the 1992 reimposition found that between 1986 and 1989 basic cable rates rose by an average 39 to 43 percent, depending on the definition of basic service.[23] Rates rose more sharply in systems that were regulated before 1986 (47 percent) than in those that were not regulated (32 percent), suggesting that regulation had been a binding constraint.[24] Average revenues per subscriber grew by only 21 percent from 1986 to 1989, largely because premium cable rates did not grow and the number of subscriptions to the premium channels decreased. Channel capacity grew from an average of thirty-four in November 1986 to forty in December 1989. Average revenues per channel remained virtually constant in nominal dollars but fell in real (inflation-adjusted) dollars.[25]

In the wake of the GAO's findings, public pressure began to build for tighter regulation of cable services. The FCC responded in 1991 by tightening its definition of effective competition; it required the availability of at least six unduplicated local off-air broadcast stations for cable systems to avoid rate regulation.[26] The commission defended this tighter definition as being justified by the greater channel capacity of cable television and the consequent larger number of consumer alternatives that would have to be available to provide effective competition. At the same time, Congress was drafting legislation to reimpose rate regulation. In 1992 the Cable Television Act was passed over President Bush's veto. After just six years of deregulation, the cable industry was now subject to both federal and municipal regulation of rates.

But this reregulation was not simply a return to the rather casual oversight of rates and services once undertaken by most municipalities. Regulation would now be supervised by the FCC in accordance with the strict instructions of the new legislation. Formal definitions of what constituted effective competition were provided by the 1992 act. Cost-of-service as-

---

22. The details of this regulatory regime are provided in chapter 2.

23. General Accounting Office, *Follow-Up National Survey*. This study followed up the GAO's August 1989 study, *National Survey of Cable Television Rates and Services*, GAO/RCED 89-193.

24. In appendix A, we find through a two-stage least-squares model that systems subject to rate regulation in 1986 showed rate increases through 1992 that were 5 percent greater than the increases for systems not subject to regulation.

25. General Accounting Office, *Follow-Up National Survey*, pp. 57, 61.

26. 6 FCC Rcd 4545 (1991).

sessments would be provided for cable system owners who demanded them in efforts to raise rates. Strict rules on passing new costs along to subscribers would be established, as would rules for allowing the costs of affiliated program networks to be passed through. The FCC would be allowed to set rates for improvements to various levels or tiers of service if sufficient numbers of consumers complained about the quality of service. To administer the new regulations, the FCC would need hundreds of new staff, and state and local governments would potentially need thousands. Cable companies would have to hire thousands more to comply with the new rules.[27] Following closely on the heels of transportation, financial services, and even partial telephone rate *deregulation,* this resurgence of legislated regulation was a remarkable change in direction, one that motivated this book.

The Changing Structure of Cable Television

The cable television industry has evolved from a collection of locally owned small franchises offering no original programming to large multiple system operators that are national entertainment companies. These MSOs not only own a large number of cable franchises, but they have interests in a variety of entertainment ventures, including cable program networks. The very size of these companies and their potential control over program content have created some concern among Washington policymakers.

Horizontal Integration

As the cable television industry grew, ownership became more concentrated. In 1975, for example, when cable was still limited in its ability to carry premium services or import distant signals, the ten largest multiple system operators controlled systems serving 40 percent of all subscribers. By 1990, when the number of subscribers had increased fivefold, the ten largest MSOs served 62 percent.[28] The single largest, TeleCommunications Inc. (TCI), reached 28 percent. By the end of 1994 fourteen MSOs, each

27. In addition to hiring new staff, cable operators would spend tens of millions of dollars on legal, accounting, and other outside professionals to comply with regulations and to challenge local, state, and federal rulemaking. The Telecommunications Act of 1996 removes some of these regulatory requirements, but most remain. See the discussion below.

28. 5 FCC Rcd 4962 (1990).

Table 1-2. *Largest Cable Television Multiple System Owners, 1995*

Owner	Subscribers	Owner	Subscribers
TeleCommunications Inc.	11,494,000	Cablevision Industries	1,396,000
Time Warner Cable	7,504,000	Jones Intercable	1,323,000
Comcast	3,320,000	Times Mirror Cable	1,314,000
Continental Cablevision	3,081,000	Television	
Cablevision Systems	2,635,000	Viacom Cable	1,139,000
Cox Communications	1,852,000	Sammons Communications	1,101,000
Newhouse Broadcasting	1,425,000	Falcon Cable TV	1,054,000
Adelphia Communications	1,407,000	Century Communications	955,000

Source: National Cable Television Association, *Cable Television Developments*, vol. 19 (Washington, Spring 1995), p. 14.

with 1 million or more basic cable customers, collectively accounted for 72 percent of all subscribers (table 1-2).

The national concentration of ownership has been propelled in part by the need to raise large amounts of capital to build urban cable systems and to incorporate the continual improvements in technology. Small cable systems are too lightly capitalized to invest the hundreds of millions of dollars required to wire a metropolitan area. In addition, today's cable industry does far more than transmit broadcast signals; indeed, programming and packaging have become the most lucrative activities. Large MSOs can negotiate for programming more efficiently and pass it along at lower prices than smaller systems can. Vertical integration between program production and cable distribution also allows for some reduction of risk in program development. Small independent cable systems simply cannot develop their own programming.

Program Supply

The cable industry has developed a wide array of new programming to be delivered over its networks, a term that had a more literal meaning during the era in which terrestrial broadcasting was dominant. A cable network is simply a program service that delivers a continuous or nearly continuous stream of programs over a single satellite transponder to cable systems throughout the country.[29] These networks are generally categorized as providing basic, premium, or pay-per-view services. Basic net-

---

29. Even this defintion of cable network is restrictive. Some networks are exploring the development of terrestrial fiber-optic grids for distribution; others are using noncable outlets such as direct broadcast satellites. See chapter 5.

works are offered by cable systems as part of their primary programming services.[30] These services may be paid for entirely by cable systems' revenues from subscribers' monthly fees, by advertising, or by both. Premium services are offered to subscribers individually for a separate monthly fee. They provide a mixture of recent motion pictures, live entertainment, and live sports. Pay-per-view services offer dozens of events or motion pictures every month, each for a separate fee to a subscriber who generally must lease a converter that activates (or unscrambles) the channel when the subscriber orders the program.

One glance at the programming provided by the basic cable networks listed in table 1-3 shows the new focuses opened up by expanding channel capacity. Networks specialize in old feature films, home shopping, travel reports, weather reports, gospel music, live coverage of Congress, financial news, Hispanic programming, and many other subjects. To expand their subscriber rosters, systems must appeal to a variety of tastes not satisfied by the four off-air broadcast networks, independent television stations, and public television. Recent improvements in technology have allowed most systems to expand their offerings to at least 50 channels, and new digital signal compression techniques may allow as many as 500 to be delivered over a single cable.[31] To fill these channels, cable operators may now choose from among more than 100 basic cable, 12 national premium, 11 pay-per-view networks, and a number of regional broadcast networks, particularly those carrying local sports teams. All but a few of these were launched after 1979, their development spurred by the deregulation of the FCC's restrictions governing cable signal carriage, the reversal of the rules restricting premium channels, and subsequent municipal rate deregulation.

In addition, cable systems generally carry all local off-air broadcast signals and many carry broadcast signals from nearby markets. They may also offer locally originated programming, including programs from local governments and schools. Thus although most U.S. cable systems can offer fifty channels, the number of programming alternatives from which they may choose continues to be several times that capacity.

30. The 1992 Cable Act invented the term *cable programming services* to refer to all nonpremium programming services beyond the basic tier. Before the 1992 act, most of these services were packaged in tiers commonly called *expanded basic* or *enhanced basic,* terms still in use in the cable market.

31. These large-capacity systems will deliver a stream of digital bits that will have to be decoded by either a digital receiver or a converter attached to the current analog receivers.

Table 1-3. *National Cable Television Networks, 1995*

Network	Type of programming	Date launched
	Basic	
All News Channel	News	1989
America's Talking	Talk	1994
American Movie Classics	Old movies	1984
Arts & Entertainment	Arts	1984
ANA Television	Arab-American	Unknown
Asian American Satellite TV	Chinese language	1992
Black Entertainment TV	Black programming	1980
Bravo	Arts and entertainment	1980
Cable Health Club	Exercise, health	1993
Canal de Noticias NBC	Spanish language	1993
Canal Sur	Latin American	1991
The Cartoon Network	Cartoons	1992
Catalog 1	Home shopping	1994
Channel America Television	Sports, music, talk	1988
Classic Arts Showcase	Arts	1994
Country Music Television	Country music	1983
CNBC	Business, talk	1989
c/net: The Computer Network	Computers, on-line services	1995
CNN	News	1980
CNN Headline News	News	1982
CNN International	Global news	1995
Comedy Central	Comedy	1991
Consumer Resource Network	Consumer information	1994
Courtroom Television Network	Courtroom trials	1991
The Crime Channel	Crime prevention	1993
C-SPAN	Public affairs	1979
CSPAN-II	Public affairs	1986
Deep Dish TV	Educational	1986
Discovery Channel	Educational	1985
E! Entertainment Television	Entertainment news	1990
ESPN	Sports	1979
ESPN2	Sports	1993
EWTN: The Catholic Cable Network	Religious	1981
Faith and Values Channel	Religious	1993 (merger)
The Family Channel	Entertainment	1977
FoxNet	Fox Television Network	1991
fX	Entertainment	1994
fXM: Movies from Fox	Motion pictures	1994
Galavision	Spanish language	1979
Game Show Network	Game shows	1994
GEMS International Television	Spanish language for women	1993
The History Channel	History, documentaries	1995
Home & Garden Television	Advice on entertaining, home repair, gardening	1994
Home Shopping Network I	Home shopping	1985
Home Shopping Network II	Home shopping	1986
The Idea Channel	Information	1992

Table 1-3. *(continued)*

Network	Type of programming	Date launched
The Inspirational Network	Religious, entertainment	1978
International Channel	Multiethnic	1990
Jewish Television Network	Jewish	1981
Jones Computer Network	Instructional	1994
Kaleidoscope	Disabled persons	1990
KTLA/UV	Superstation	1988
Ladbroke Racing Channel	Horse racing	1984
The Learning Channel	Educational	1980
Lifetime Television	Women's programming	1984
Mind Extension University	Educational	1987
MOR Music TV	Music	1992
MTV: Music Television	Music	1981
MTV: Latino	Spanish-language music	1993
MuchMusic USA	Music	1994
NASA Television	Public affairs, space	1980
NET—Political NewsTalk Network	Public affairs	1993
Network One	Entertainment	1993
Newstalk Television	News, interactive	1994
Newsworld International	News	1994
Nick at Nite	Entertainment	1985
Nickleodeon	Children's entertainment	1979
The 90s Channel	Documentaries	1989
Nostalgia Television	Entertainment	1985
Prime SportsChannel	Sports	1993
Product Information Network	Infomercials	1994
QVC	Shopping	1986
Q2	Shopping	1994
SciFi Channel	Science fiction	1992
SCOLA	Educational	1987
Shop At Home	Shopping	1986
Singlevision	Entertainment, information	1994
TBS	Superstation	1976
Telemundo	Spanish programming	1987
Television Food Network	Food	1993
TNN	Country music	1983
TNT	Entertainment	1988
The Travel Channel	Travel	1987
Trinity Broadcasting Network	Religious	1973
Trio	Family entertainment	1994
Turner Classic Movies	Movies	1994
U Network	Student-produced programs	1989
Univision	Hispanic	1976
USA Network	Entertainment	1980
ValueVision	Shopping	1991
VH1	Music	1985
Via TV Network	Shopping	1993
Video Catalog Channel	Shopping	1991
The Weather Channel	Weather	1982
WGN/UV	Superstation	1978
The Worship Network	Religious music	1992

Table 1-3. *(continued)*

Network	Type of programming	Date launched
WPIX/UPI	Superstation	1984
WSBK	Superstation	1988
WWOR/EMI	Superstation	1979
Z Music	Music	1993
	Premium	
Cinemax	Motion pictures, etc.	1980
The Disney Channel	Filmed entertainment	1983
Encore	Motion pictures	1991
The Filipino Channel	Filipino programming	1994
Flix	Motion pictures	1992
The Golf Channel	Golf	1995
HBO	Motion pictures, etc.	1972
The Independent Film Channel	Motion pictures, etc.	1994
Playboy	Adult programming	1982
The Movie Channel	Motion pictures, etc.	1979
Showtime	Motion pictures, etc.	1976
TV Asia	Asian programming	1993
TV-JAPAN	Japanese language	1991
	Pay-per-view	
Action Pay Per View	Action, adventure	1990
Adam and Eve	Adult	1994
Cable Video Store	Motion pictures	1986
Cine Latino	Spanish language	1994
Request Television[a]	Motion pictures, etc.	1985
Spice	Adult	1989
Viewer's Choice	Motion pictures, etc.	1985
Viewer's Choice: Continuous Hits[b]	Motion pictures, etc.	1993
Viewer's Choice: Hot Choice	Action-adventure motion pictures	1986
Viva Television Network	Spanish language	1993

Source: National Cable Television Association, *Cable Television Developments*, vol. 19 (Spring 1995), pp. 25–75.
a. Offers five separate services.
b. Offers three separate services.

Vertical Integration

Filling the rapidly expanding number of channels with services that subscribers might value is obviously a challenging and risky activity. Few investors are willing to undertake such ventures without some prior commitment from cable system owners. As a result, TCI, Time Warner, Cox Cable, and other large system operators have been major investors in cable networks in the past fifteen years. At the end of 1992, fifteen of the largest twenty-five networks were owned wholly or in part by MSOs (table 1-4). Innovative networks such as Black Entertainment Television, Lifetime,

Table 1-4. *Cable Television Network Multiple System Operator Ownership in Twenty-Five Largest Basic Cable Networks, December 1992*

Network	Percent of subscribers reached	MSO with interest	Date launched
ESPN	99.0	None	1979
CNN	98.7	TCI, Time Warner, Viacom, and others	1980
TBS	96.8	TCI, Time Warner, Viacom, and others	1976
USA Network	96.8	None	1980
The Discovery Channel	95.2	TCI, Newhouse, Cox	1985
Nickelodeon/Nick at Nite	94.7	Viacom (100 percent)	1979
CSPAN[a]	94.4	...	1979
TNT	94.0	TCI, Time Warner, Viacom, and others	1988
MTV	92.4	Viacom (100 percent)	1981
The Family Channel	92.3	TCI	1977
The Nashville Network	91.8	None	1983
Lifetime	91.5	Viacom	1984
Arts and Entertainment	90.5	None	1984
The Weather Channel	86.0	None	1982
Headline News	82.9	TCI, Time Warner, Viacom, and others	1982
CNBC	76.9	None	1989
VH-1	76.0	Viacom (100 percent)	1985
QVC Network	71.8	TCI, Time Warner, Comcast	1986
American Movie Classics	69.4	TCI, Cablevision Systems	1984
WGN/UVI	61.5	None	1978
Black Entertainment Television	55.3	TCI, Time Warner	1980
CSPAN-II[a]	47.3	...	1986
EWTN: The Catholic Cable Network	46.8	None	1981
Comedy Central	43.5	Time Warner, Viacom	1991
Mind Extension University	37.1	Jones Intercable	1987

Source: David H. Waterman and Andrew A. Weiss, *Vertical Integration in Cable Television* (Washington: American Enterprise Institute, 1993), tables 2-2, 2-3.

a. Cable affiliates provide 95 percent of funding but have no ownership interests or program control.

The Discovery Channel, and the Family Channel were developed with MSO investment.

This vertical integration has been controversial because it is alleged to hinder systems using new distribution technologies such as direct broadcast satellites (DBS) or multichannel, multipoint distribution services (MMDS) from entering the market. The FCC concluded in 1990 that the integration had resulted in a greater investment in new networks.[32] It recommended, however, that Congress consider legislating against some of the more egregious ways by which cable system operators might shut out competitive media, a recommendation carried out in the 1992 Cable Act.[33]

Do MSOs use their ownership interests in cable networks to dampen competition? There are two arguments that they do. The first asserts that they deny new entrants into video distribution access to essential programming. The second suggests that vertically integrated MSOs favor cable networks in which they have an interest or discriminate against those in which they have no such interest.

The argument that MSOs use their vertical integration to deny new cable distribution technologies access to critical programming ignores some vital details. No single MSO owns a large enough share of enough networks to be able to determine new competitors' success or failure, nor does any one MSO typically control even one network in which it has an interest. There is, for instance, no cable system ownership of ESPN, perhaps the most popular basic cable network, and one that any new system would want to carry. The two MSOs (Time Warner and TCI) with interests in the second most popular network, CNN, together own only 40 percent.[34] There are a few networks in which MSOs have more than a 50 percent interest, but most, such as Comedy Central or The Learning Channel, are specialized. Others include home shopping channels and music video channels, which can be duplicated rather easily and are now proliferating.

To use control of programming to exclude new system operators, MSOs would have to own far larger shares of more channels, collude with one another, or do both. Collusion would be difficult to carry out without detection by antitrust authorities. It has been suggested, however, that the current extent of vertical integration could allow cable operators to exclude potential competitors without collusion. TCI or Time Warner could threaten not to carry a new network to discourage rivals from developing their own basic networks that compete with those in which the MSO has

32. 5 FCC Rcd 4962 (1990).

33. 5 FCC Rcd 4962 (1990), para. 130. The 1992 act requires the FCC to establish rules governing the number of channels on a cable system that may carry programming in which the cable system has an interest. Such rules would potentially limit how much cable system owners could engage in producing video programming and would ensure that cable operators with ownership interests in programming do not favor their programming nor engage in discriminatory practices in distributing it to competing distribution media (sec.11(c)).

34. David H. Waterman and Andrew A. Weiss, *Vertical Integration in Cable Television* (Washington: American Enterprise Institute, 1993), p. 9.

an interest. Several well-publicized incidents suggest that such power may be used on occasion. In 1985, before acquiring its interest in CNN, TCI is alleged to have encouraged NBC's attempt to start a new cable news network in order to gain leverage over the rates charged by CNN. But once CNN cut its rates, TCI discouraged NBC. In 1990, it was alleged, TCI induced the Lifetime Network to drop its bid for The Learning Channel by threatening to drop the channel from its systems if Lifetime succeeded. Lifetime apparently withdrew its bid, and a TCI subsidiary subsequently purchased TLC.[35]

The second argument linking vertical integration to monopoly power focuses on cable programming rather than video distribution. Through vertical integration, it is alleged, large MSOs can prevent entry into cable programming because they favor their own programming and are less likely to purchase programming in which they have no financial interest. Once again, however, the fact is that no MSO controls systems accounting for more than 22 percent of cable subscribers.[36] Given the number of cable networks that survive even though they serve less than 50 percent of cable subscribers (table 1-4 provides some examples), it is difficult to see how entry could be frustrated unless the MSOs colluded. And once again, ESPN, USA Network, and other successful networks have no MSO interest. Finally, the entry of new networks, both with and without MSO interests, does not seem to have slowed. Indeed, fully 20 percent of all basic networks listed in table 1-3 were launched in 1994 and 1995.

There are a fair number of studies on what networks the cable systems decide to carry.[37] In general, they conclude that an MSO's financial interest in a network increases the probability that its systems will carry the network but that the effects of this are not very important. There is no evidence that MSOs discriminate against basic cable networks they do not own. Nor do most vertically integrated systems carry significantly fewer basic cable

---

35. Waterman and Weiss, "Vertical Integration in Cable Television," pp. 41–42. The authors point out that a private antitrust suit was unsuccessful in the former case. No antitrust action was brought in the second.

36. Waterman and Weiss, "Vertical Integration in Cable Television," p. 13.

37. See Benjamin Klein, "The Competitive Consequences of Vertical Integration in the Cable Industry," paper prepared for the National Cable Television Association, University of California at Los Angeles, June 1989; Michael A. Salinger, "A Test of Successive Monopoly and Foreclosure Effects: Vertical Integration between Cable Systems and Pay Services," Columbia University working paper, 1988; Robert W. Crandall, "Vertical Integration and q Ratios in the Cable Industry," paper prepared for TCI, 1990, in MM docket no. 89-600; and Waterman and Weiss, "Vertical Integration in Cable Television."

networks than nonintegrated systems.[38] Finally, there is considerable evidence that the two major premium networks, HBO (owned by Warner-ATC) and Showtime (owned by Viacom), are more likely to be carried by systems controlled by the MSO that owns the network and less likely to be carried by systems controlled by the MSO owning the other network.

Assuming that these observations are correct, they do not, by themselves, suggest that vertical integration reduces viewers' welfare by reducing their program choices. Without vertical integration, the number of choices might be much smaller, even if cable systems had no incentive to favor one network over another for reasons other than subscriber demand. The fact that MSO-owned systems favor their own networks is hardly surprising given the public-goods nature of cable programming and the difficulty in fashioning efficient contracts to ensure that nonintegrated systems carry all networks whose marginal value is greater than the next best alternative. Therefore, studies showing MSOs' favoritism for carrying networks in which they have a financial stake may reveal little more than the rationality of the companies' managements or the difficulty in negotiating efficient contracts, or both. Given the continuing entry of new networks into the market, it would appear that if MSOs have attempted to monopolize programming, they have been remarkably unsuccessful.

Cable Television and the Information Superhighway

Because cable television now passes more than 95 percent of all households and serves subscribers in more than 60 percent, it is a powerful potential entrant into other communications markets.[39] The local cable system's broadband drop line into subscribers' homes or offices has far greater communications capacity than the paired copper wires of the telephone company.[40] This advantage is usually offset, however, by the tree-and-branch network (figure 1-1) designed to deliver one-way video and in some cases a limited amount of return traffic for ordering pay-per-view services or

---

38. Waterman and Weiss, *Vertical Integration in Cable Television,* table 4-4, find that vertical integration leads to a maximum reduction of about 0.6 basic network and a total reduction of 1.0 network (basic plus premium plus pay-per-view) carried on systems with fifty-four or more channels.

39. Paul Kagan Associates, *Kagan Media Index,* 1995.

40. Digital signal compression has increased the potential capacity of most telecommunications transmission and distribution systems, but it has not narrowed the difference in capacity between coaxial cable and paired copper wires.

otherwise signaling the cable headend (the primary distributor). Telephone networks are so-called star networks that provide the opportunity for every customer to communicate with every other customer on the network (figure 1-1). If cable television systems are to enter the traditional voice and data telephone markets or provide interactive video services, they will have to be reconfigured and switching capacity added so that messages can be directed to individual recipients.

Recent technological developments are driving cable and telephone networks toward the same configuration. Cable networks are replacing coaxial cable feeders with fiber-optic lines. As the fiber lines radiate farther from the headend, their greater capacity allows cable system operators to consider converting to the switched-network architecture telephone companies use.[41] Similarly, telephone companies are replacing their copper feeder lines with fiber optics and are beginning to contemplate creating networks of fiber-optic and coaxial cable so that they can deliver both video and traditional voice and data services. In a few years both cable and telephone networks may have the hybrid topology shown in figure 1-1, particularly in large urban areas.[42] For the immediate future, however, most cable systems will be confined to offering one-way video services and a limited amount of business data traffic in large cities.

Of perhaps greater importance is the development of digital signal-compression technologies that will allow traditional one-way cable networks to offer as many as 500 channels. Although the protocol for MPEG2, the most ambitious of these new technologies, is not yet defined sufficiently for equipment that uses it to be on the market, cable programmers are already beginning to develop strategies for exploiting the new capacity.

Cable Growth through New Services

Because cable television already reaches so many U.S. households, future growth of the medium must increasingly come from new sources of reve-

41. In early 1995 Cablevision negotiated access and interconnection agreements with NYNEX so that customers of certain Cablevision systems on Long Island could be offered telephony services that would compete with those offered by the local telephone company. Service is expected to begin as this book goes to press. Similar agreements are likely to be negotiated by many cable systems as local telephone companies are forced to unbundle their packages and offer interconnection to competing terrestrial carriers such as cable companies.

42. Pacific Bell announced its intention to begin replacing its telephone plant in major metropolitan markets in California with a hybrid network similar to that shown in figure 1-1, but slowed implementation of the plan in 1995.

Figure 1-1. Communications Distribution Networks[a]

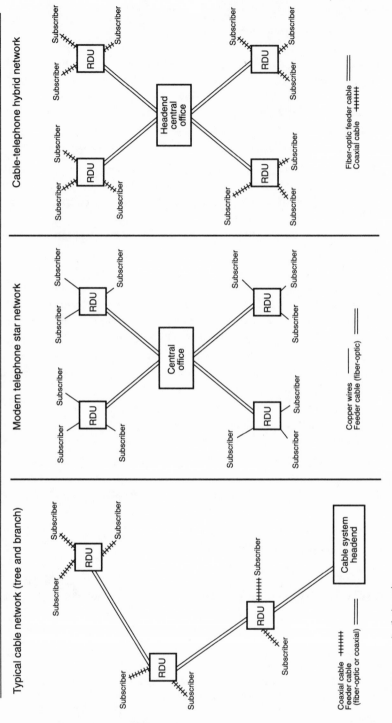

a. RDU is remote distribution unit.

nue provided by its existing subscriber base. Indeed, if direct broadcast satellites, broadband telephone networks, or other new technologies are successful, cable subscriptions could even decrease. Both cable operators and companies using these technologies will thus be searching for new services and programming ideas to attract subscribers, particularly in the face of dramatic increases in channel capacity.

One possibility for expanding the demand for cable service lies in pay-per-view or video-on-demand services, particularly those offering motion pictures. At present, cable subscribers' choices of feature films at any given hour are limited to the selections available on HBO, Showtime, or other premium channels or those on basic cable networks or commercial broadcast stations. Pay-per-view services are still in their infancy, in part because of the paucity of addressable converters that allow the system to communicate with a given subscriber, a service often referred to as video on demand or the video jukebox. With many more channels, consumer choices could be greatly expanded. HBO could offer the same two-hour film on perhaps eight channels with starts staggered fifteen minutes apart. Or the eight channels could offer eight very different lineups of movies.[43] Finally, a network could be designed to allow subscribers to order any film at any time, an order that could be filled by reading the film off a disk stored at the cable system's headend or at a remote video server facility for switched delivery to the subscriber. This would permit subscribers to use a library of taped material in much the same way as they now use rented video tapes. Program material could be stopped, fast-forwarded, or repeated at the viewer's discretion.

Other ideas being explored include upscale shopping, high-speed interactive services such as medical diagnostics, a form of video telephony, on-line computer games, and travel services. Given the likely explosion in channel capacity and rapidly declining costs of electronics, the array of potential offerings is very large, as is the risk of developing any that prove to be unwanted by subscribers. And many new services may require completely different network architectures to allow for full two-way video communication among subscribers. If cable systems wish to enter the market for interactive, two-way services they will have to reconfigure their systems, which will be expensive.[44] As table 1-5 shows, the market for home video offerings is still dominated by basic and premium cable, traditional

43. The new direct broadcast satellite service, DirecTV, offers pay-per-view movies on eighty to one hundred channels.
44. We address the subjects of competition and the cost of alternative architectures in chapter 5.

Table 1-5. *Revenue from Home Video Services, by Source, 1994*[a]

Sources	Revenue (billions of dollars)
Consumer expenditures for Home Video Services	
Basic cable	14.995
Premium cable	4.963
Pay-per-view	0.668
Home video rentals and purchases	14.398
Total	35.024
Home video advertising	
Broadcasting	30.267
Cable	4.607
Barter	1.511
Total	36.385
Total home video services (excluding home shopping)	71.409
Home shopping	2.838
Total home video services	74.247

Source: *Kagan Media Index*, April 24, 1995.
a. Table reflects a relatively narrow definition of home video services. Excluded are consumer purchases of on-line computer and information services, purchases and rentals of video equipment, purchases and advertiser support of audio services, and purchases of computer software and games.

broadcasting, and home video sales and rentals. Pay-per-view, home shopping, and other services accounted for less than 5 percent of all video revenues in 1994.

The Outlook

Cable television is now buffeted by two forces. On the one hand, it is regulated as a local monopoly and subject to limitations on the rates it can charge and the programming services it can own. Some of the provisions of the 1992 act have been relaxed by the Telecommunications Act of 1996, but cable operators still face a daunting array of complex federal regulations. On the other, it will be challenged by new technologies for delivering video signals to the home. Direct broadcast satellites are beginning to offer scores of channels of programming. A cellular cable service is pioneering in New York. And telephone companies, particularly the regional Bell operating companies, are building new broadband capacity in preparation for offering cable television and other innovative services. Some MSOs and telephone companies have pursued alliances with each other to develop their cable systems into more complete, two-way networks able to compete for the full array of voice, data, and video services. But many of these joint ventures or outright mergers were negotiated just as the FCC was beginning to implement the 1992 Cable Act. When the commission's rules were announced, particularly those affecting subscriber rates that were released in early 1994, the largest of these joint ventures were quickly abandoned.[45]

As one growth prospect, cable operators are exploring narrowband voice-data services to complement their broadband video services. And a motivating force behind the Bell operating companies' drive to form joint ventures with cable companies is their desire to compete with other telephone companies in offering traditional voice-data connections to subscribers outside their own regions. Cable companies are actively pursuing alliances with wireless telephone carriers as one way to enter the switched voice-telephony market. Many of these ventures are constrained, however, by cable regulation and state telephone regulation.

45. Bell Atlantic had offered to buy TCI, the largest cable system owner, and Southwestern Bell had proposed to buy 40 percent of Cox Cable.

CHAPTER TWO

Cable Rate Regulation

REGULATION is a political process. It may be motivated by a desire to increase general economic welfare, consumer welfare, producer welfare, or the incomes of favored groups in the population.[1] The popular notion that regulation is an efficient antidote for natural monopoly is contradicted by several generations of economic studies of transportation, energy, financial, and communications markets.[2] Moreover, monopoly, natural or unnatural, is neither a necessary nor a sufficient condition to explain the legislative proclivity to regulate an industry.

In the case of cable television, regulation has been justified as part of a municipal licensing regime, as a component of a wider communications policy designed to stimulate and protect traditional broadcasting, and most recently as a corrective for supposedly unwarranted increases in charges to subscribers. Until the late 1970s the industry was restrained in order to promote the growth of traditional television broadcasting, particularly that by local independent stations.[3] In 1984 Congress sought to remove cable systems from the stranglehold of municipal rate regulation as long as the FCC ascertained that they faced effective competition. In 1992 Congress reconsidered and launched a long, laborious process of instituting multiple layers of centralized rate regulation, ostensibly because of consumer complaints that cable operators had raised rates excessively under deregulation. In 1996 Congress removed some of those provisions but left the basic structure of federal legislation intact.

Since passage of the Cable Television Consumer Protection and Competition Act of 1992, and continuing after the passage of the Telecommunica-

---

1. For an empirical investigation into the politics of regulation, see Clifford Winston and Robert W. Crandall, "Explaining Regulatory Policy," *Brookings Papers on Economic Activity: Microeconomics, 1994*, pp. 1–32.

2. For a survey of this literature, see Clifford Winston, "Economic Deregulation: Days of Reckoning for Microeconomists," *Journal of Economic Literature*, vol. 31 (September 1993), pp. 1263–89.

3. For a discussion of the early period of regulation and deregulation, see chapter 1 and Stanley M. Besen and Robert W. Crandall, "The Deregulation of Cable Television," *Law and Contemporary Problems*, vol. 44 (Winter 1981), pp. 77–124.

tions Act of 1996, the apparent goal of cable regulation has been to reduce consumer rates for basic services without any concern for the effects on viewing choices or investment in new technologies.[4] In this chapter we examine the likely effects of such regulation on cable rates, service quality, the value of franchises, and other variables that are important in measuring consumer and producer welfare.

The Rationale for Rate Regulation

Congressional proponents justified the 1992 Cable Act as a means to control monopoly power. Relying on the surveys conducted by the General Accounting Office, they argued that cable companies had raised prices out of proportion to cost increases since the end of 1986 when the 1984 rate deregulation became effective.[5] But between November 1986 and the end of 1989 these companies had also increased the average number of channels offered by more than 25 percent and had greatly expanded the diversity and value of the programming.[6] The number of national cable networks expanded from forty-eight in 1984 to seventy-eight in 1988.[7] Rates did rise by 43 percent from 1986 to 1989, but did the increases reflect monopoly power or simply the necessary costs of attracting and distributing new programming?

It is certainly possible that cable television was not a competitive or even a contestable market in 1992. To analyze the extent of competition, we

---

4. Before enactment of the 1992 act, basic or enhanced basic services referred to the standard packages of programming that cable operators required subscribers to purchase before they could buy access to HBO and other premium cable channels. The 1992 act introduced new terminology, dividing *basic services* into *basic service* and *cable programming services*. Unless otherwise noted, we will use the earlier common definition and refer to all programming packages other than premium channels as basic services.

5. See General Accounting Office, *National Survey of Cable Television Rates and Services,* GAO/RCED 89-193 (August 1989); and *Follow-Up National Survey of Cable Television Rates and Services,* GAO/RCED 90-199 (June 1990).

6. There is an unfortunate tendency to overlook the changes that have occurred in cable programming. Cable news channels have become more numerous and specialized. Premium channels have increased the number of original programs instead of relying on repeats of theatrical-quality motion pictures. Pay-per-view services have allowed subscribers to choose among a wider variety of programs.

7. National Cable Television Association, *Cable Television Developments,* vol. 19 (Spring 1995), p. 7.

begin with a definition of the market. Cable television provides a variety of entertainment, information, and even home shopping programming. Similar services may be obtained from local television stations, satellite retransmissions, local sports teams, movie theaters, video rentals, newspapers, magazines, radio stations, and retail shops.[8] If entertainment constitutes a separate market, this list becomes shorter. If video entertainment is separate, the list shrinks a great deal more, and if home video is separate it shrinks even further.[9]

Economists typically refer to a combination of product markets and geographic markets to examine whether a firm does or could exercise some power to raise prices above competitive levels. A product market is a group of goods or services whose availability and prices discipline one another. Where are the boundaries of the product market in which cable television services compete? The question has not been answered, even by the Federal Communications Commission.[10] The Cable Act of 1992 focuses narrowly on multichannel means of video distribution as the product market, to the exclusion of such single-channel means as broadcast television signals and movie rentals. In requiring price regulation under the act, Congress ignored a decade of evidence that the availability of clear broadcast signals affects the ability of cable operators to raise prices.[11] In 1994 in its first annual review of video markets, the commission acknowledged the potential for broadcast signals to reduce cable subscription charges, but in deference to the 1992 act adopted "multichannel video programming service"

8. Home satellite dishes, generally three to six feet in diameter, may receive cable programming directly without the intervention of a cable operator. In addition, direct broadcast satellite services have appeared, offering one hundred channels or more to subscribers who purchase smaller (eighteen-inch) satellite receivers.

9. We are not aware of any definitive evidence supporting a market definition as inclusive as all information and entertainment services or as narrow as home video entertainment. Not surprisingly, the FCC has defined markets so as to be consistent with legislative mandates for cable rate regulation rather than with economic evidence. See, for example, 9 FCC Rcd 7442 (1994). As legislative mandates have changed, so have the FCC market definitions. Under the 1984 Cable Act, over-the-air broadcast signals formed the primary source of "effective competition." Under the 1992 Cable Act, these single-channel signals do not influence market definition; only multichannel video distribution systems count.

10. American Bar Association Antitrust Section, *The 1992 Horizontal Merger Guidelines: Commentary and Text* (Washington, 1992).

11. With its 1992 database the FCC did test for an effect of broadcast signals on cable prices but found none; see 9 FCC Rcd 4119 (1994). The absence of an effect announced in this document contrasted with the findings and conclusions reached as recently as 1991 in 6 FCC Rcd 4545 (1991).

as the relevant product market.[12] Yet in a separate but contemporaneous proceeding, the FCC defined a broader market of "delivered video programming," one in which broadcast stations compete on an equal footing with cable operators.[13]

Unfettered by regulation, a cable operator will charge prices for its services that maximize its profit. These prices will always be on the quality-adjusted demand curves for those services, but the cable operator can choose among alternative price levels, depending on the extent of competition. A perfectly competitive market will yield a price no higher than marginal cost, and a contestable market will yield an equilibrium price no higher than average cost.[14] A purely monopolistic market will yield a price no higher than the position on the demand curve immediately above the intersection of marginal revenue and marginal cost. Within a market, *market power*—the extent to which prices exceed marginal cost—is limited by competing sources of supply.[15]

One of the principal findings of Congress in passing the Cable Act of 1992 was not merely that cable operators exercised market power, presumably for basic service, but that "undue market power" resulted from an absence of effective competition.[16] Neither market power nor undue market power is defined in the act.[17]

12. 9 FCC Rcd 7442 (1994).

13. 10 FCC Rcd 3524 (1995).

14. See William J. Baumol, John C. Panzar, and Robert D. Willig, *Contestable Markets and the Theory of Industry Structure* (Harcourt Brace Jovanovich, 1982).

15. Market power is usually associated with a price higher than marginal cost even for a business with average cost in excess of marginal cost. Businesses may set prices at or below average cost and still be defined as having some market power. See Jean Tirole, *The Theory of Industrial Organization* (MIT Press, 1988), p. 284. Cable operators have large fixed costs and are therefore likely to confront average costs that are greater than marginal costs.

16. "Without the presence of another multichannel video programming distributor, a cable system faces no local competition. The result is undue market power for the cable operator as compared to that of consumers and video programmers." *Cable Television Consumer Protection and Competition Act of 1992*, sec.2(a)(2).

17. The usage may simply mean pricing above average cost or above prices charged by the lowest-priced services in the industry. The act seems to make no direct link between market power and marginal cost. To the extent that some or all cable operators operate with average costs above marginal costs, marginal cost prices for basic cable services might be observed in the short run, but they would not be sustainable in the long run. Under these conditions cable operators have market power inasmuch as they price above marginal cost; to the extent that prices remain in the range of average costs, however, there are no supranormal profits. See Tirole, *Theory of Industrial Organization*, p. 284.

The finding that cable operators exercised market power, apparently based on 1989 and 1990 studies by the General Accounting Office, was not rooted in consistent results from empirical research. In its implementation of the 1984 act the FCC had decided that effective competition existed as long as a cable system faced competition from at least three local television broadcast signals. The General Accounting Office found that as of the end of 1989 this rule had the effect of exempting 96.5 percent of cable systems from rate regulation.[18] In 1991, partly in response to public concern over rising rates, the commission revised the standard for effective competition so that it required at least six broadcast signals. The justification for this change was that cable systems had so expanded the number of channels they offered that three local signals were no longer sufficient to prevent operators from exploiting monopoly power.[19]

The strength of cable's monopoly has been debated at great length.[20] Proponents of reining in system operators often emphasize that the q ratios for cable stocks, the ratio of their market value to the cost of building them, are far in excess of one, reflecting purported market power.[21] However, this ratio reflects the market's assessment of a company's *prospective* profits from all future sources, not just the current profitability of operations.[22] No one doubts that cable companies have bright prospects in a variety of media, but this does not necessarily mean that current cable rates yield large monopoly profits. Given that cable systems have traditionally sold for eleven to twelve times cash flow, it is obvious that investors are expecting substantial growth from them, growth that is not likely to come from distributive (one-way) cable services alone.[23]

Rates for basic cable service may be lower in markets in which there are two competing operators than in markets with only one. Older studies estimate 8 to 10 percent lower; more recent FCC studies, undertaken to implement the 1992 Cable Act, estimate 9 to 28 percent lower. Two recent

18. General Accounting Office, *Follow-Up National Survey,* p. 12.

19. 6 FCC Rcd 4545 (1991).

20. See comments filed in FCC proceedings in 1990, document 89-600, and 1991, 6 FCC Rcd 4545. See also Robert N. Rubinovitz, "Market Power and Price Increases for Basic Cable Service since Deregulation," *RAND Journal of Economics,* vol. 24 (Spring 1993), pp. 1–18.

21. See, for example, Paul W. MacAvoy, "Tobin's q and the Cable Industry's Market Power," in MM Docket no. 89-600, February 28, 1990, app. 5.

22. For an earlier analysis of the prospective profitability of cable television, see Robert W. Crandall, "The Profitability of Cable Television: An Examination of Acquisition Prices," *Journal of Business,* vol. 47 (October 1974), pp. 543–63.

23. Price-equity ratios are from 9 FCC Rcd 7442 (1994).

studies using two-stage least-squares techniques slightly more sophisticated than those used by the FCC suggest a differential of 20 percent.[24]

Measuring the contribution to economic welfare of an additional competitor in a market for heterogeneous services is difficult under the best circumstances. Unambiguous measures of the contribution of competition to price reductions are also elusive. For example, some analyses of the data collected by the FCC in 1992 find little basis for believing that the presence of a competing cable system contributes to lower cable rates.[25]

Congress appears to have concluded that the sharp increases in basic cable rates after deregulation in 1986 were proof of cable's market power.[26] But the increases could simply have reflected the cost (and value) of the increased quality of service or even recovery of the cost of basic service after rates had been kept at less-than-competitive levels by municipal regulation during a period of inflation. If there were an increase in cable systems' ability to exercise market power after deregulation, one might have expected the value of their stocks to rise with each congressional or FCC move toward rate deregulation in 1981–85. Yet the values of cable equities did not respond to these moves in a statistically significant manner.[27] Equity values began to respond only in 1986–88, but even this response was weak.

Perhaps the best evidence of the limited effects of deregulation on cable profitability can be found in the pattern of prices paid for cable systems in mergers and acquisitions. According to Robin Prager, these prices began to rise only after mid-1985; thus any effect of deregulation on anticipated market power was surely slow to penetrate the financial markets.[28] How-

24. For older studies, see Douglas W. Webbink, "The Impact of Regulation on Cable TV Service Prices, Channels, and Pay Tier," Bureau of Economics, Federal Trade Commission, May 1985; and Thomas W. Hazlett, "Competition vs. Franchise Monopoly in Cable Television," *Contemporary Policy Issues,* vol. 4 (April 1986), pp. 80–97. The FCC studies are 8 FCC Rcd 5631 (1993) and 9 FCC Rcd 4119 (1994). For a review of this literature, see Thomas W. Hazlett, "Regulating Cable Television Rates: An Economic Analysis," working paper (Washington: American Enterprise Institute, October, 1994). The two most recent studies are William M. Emmons III and Robin A. Prager, "The Effects of Market Structure and Ownership on Prices and Service Offerings in the U.S. Cable Television Industry," Harvard Business School, June 12, 1995; and Richard O. Beil Jr. and others, "Competition and the Price of Municipal Cable Television Services: An Empirical Study," *Journal of Regulatory Economics,* vol. 6 (1993), pp. 401–15.

25. See the discussion at p. 43.

26. *Cable Television Consumer Protection and Competition Act of 1992,* sec.2(a)(1), citing General Accounting Office, *Follow-Up National Survey.*

27. Robin A. Prager, "The Effects of Deregulating Cable Television: Evidence from the Financial Markets," *Journal of Regulatory Economics,* vol. 4 (December 1992), pp. 347–63.

28. Prager, "Effects of Deregulating Cable Television," p. 357.

ever, even these conclusions may be too strong. We have analyzed the prices of acquisitions completed between January 1983 and December 1993.[29] Specifically, we estimated a regression equation of the form

(2.1) $LP/SUB = f(LSUB/HP, LPAY/SUB, LSTOCKMKT,$

$LSUB, D84...D93),$

where LP/SUB is the natural logarithm of the price paid per existing subscriber, $LSUB/HP$ is the natural logarithm of the number of subscribers per home passed by the system, and $LPAY/SUB$ is the natural logarithm of the ratio of premium-service subscribers to basic subscribers.[30] $LSTOCKMKT$ is the natural logarithm of the level of stock market prices for the month in which the system sale closed.[31] $LSUB$ is the natural logarithm of the number of subscribers on the systems, and $D84...D93$ are dummy variables for each year after 1983.[32] All dollar amounts were transformed into 1982–84 prices by using the average consumer price index for the year. The results are reported in table 2-1.

Equation 2.1 is different from previous analyses in that it allows for the effect of rising general equity values by including a measure of the real level of stock prices. It also includes the logarithm of the share of premium-channel subscribers to all subscribers, reflecting the added value of subscribers to premium services in the subscriber base, and the logarithm of system market penetration, because one might expect systems with less penetration to have greater prospects for future growth. Finally, it also allows, through $LSUB$, for the possibility that large transactions are worth more than smaller ones because they permit economies of agglomeration

---

29. Data are from Paul Kagan Associates, *The Cable TV Financial Data Book* (Carmel, Calif.: annual editions). We took a random sample of 493 observations from the population of those reported for 1983–92, but 13 were discarded because the reported prices were far above or below the central tendency, suggesting some error in recording the price or the number of subscribers. Including these observations would have reduced the statistical precision of the estimates of the coefficients, but would not have affected the conclusion that (after correcting for the influence of the share of subscribers in the population, total subscribers, and real stock market prices) real acquisition prices did not begin to rise until 1987.

30. Specifically, it is the logarithm of the number of households subscribing to one or more premium services minus the logarithm of the number of basic subscribers.

31. Ibbotson Associates, *Stocks, Bonds, Bills, and Inflation, 1994 Yearbook* (Chicago, 1994). The Ibbotson index is a measure of the level of all stocks traded on major exchanges.

32. Data for 1994 sales are available, but the other data required to estimate equation 2.1 were not available at the time this was written.

Table 2-1. *Determinants of Real Cable System Acquisition Prices, 1983–93*[a]

Variable	1	2	3	4
Constant	−9.11	−7.93	−8.84	−8.98
	(−36.92)	(8.22)	(−40.02)	(−40.55)
LSUB/HP	−0.12	−0.11	−0.11	−0.11
(log of subscribers per home passed)	(−3.64)	(−3.28)	(−3.21)	(−3.26)
LPAY/SUB	0.016	0.011	0.0087	. . .
(log of pay subscribers per basic subscriber)	(2.96)	(1.62)	(1.56)	
LSTOCKMKT	0.32	0.043	0.21	0.22
(log of real stock market level)	(8.46)	(0.23)	(5.69)	(6.09)
LSUB	0.045	0.078	0.078	0.082
(log of the total number of basic subscribers)	(5.44)	(9.92)	(10.07)	(10.43)
D84	. . .	−0.057	. . .	. . .
		(−0.68)		
D85	. . .	−0.059	. . .	. . .
		(−0.65)		
D86	. . .	0.097	. . .	. . .
		(0.77)		
D87	. . .	0.27	0.22	0.22
		(1.80)	(6.05)	(6.08)
D88	. . .	0.40	0.36	0.37
		(2.83)	(7.20)	(7.28)
D89	. . .	0.48	0.42	0.43
		(3.03)	(9.86)	(10.09)
D90	. . .	0.42	0.35	0.36
		(2.56)	(9.08)	(9.18)
D91	. . .	0.25	0.16	0.16
		(1.32)	(4.19)	(4.20)
D92	. . .	0.15	. . .	. . .
		(0.75)		
D93	. . .	0.13	. . .	. . .
		(0.61)		
D94	. . .	0.07	. . .	. . .
		(0.032)		
$\bar{R}^2$	0.220	0.397	0.393	0.399

Source: Authors' calculations.

a. Based on 480 observations; *t*-statistics are in parentheses. The dependent variable is the natural logarithm of real price per subscriber (*LP/SUB*).

in assembling interconnected cable systems as future nodes on the information superhighway.[33]

When all the structural variables are included (without the time dummy variables), all coefficients are statistically significant at the 1 percent level

33. For cable companies to offer switched voice and data (telephony) services, they

and have the expected signs. When all the dummy variables are added, the level of real stock prices and many of the dummy variables have insignificant coefficients, probably because of collinearity. When the statistically insignificant yearly dummy variables are dropped, however, the stock market coefficient once again assumes a positive, significant coefficient (table 2-1, column 3). In most of the regressions, the coefficients of the time dummies for 1984–86 and 1992–93 prove to have statistically insignificant coefficients. These results suggest that real franchise values did not begin to rise until 1987, three years after deregulation. The results in columns 3 and 4 of table 2-1 suggest that real franchise values rose by 22 percent above their 1983–86 values in 1987 and another 20 percentage points on the original base by 1989. Thereafter, acquisition prices per subscriber receded, reaching their 1983–86 level once again in 1992–93. This finding is similar to Robin Prager's earlier aggregate result, but our more rigorous regression analysis places the turning point in 1987 rather than 1986. Thus our results suggest that two years after the 1984 Cable Act was passed, acquisition prices were still unaffected, surely an unexpected result if the act unleashed pent-up forces of monopoly power.[34]

The results shown in table 2-1 probably reflect myriad other forces. The surge in values for the systems after 1987 may have resulted from much stronger demand for cable services than the market had been expecting. The receding values in the 1990s may reflect anticipation of FCC reregulation and the decision to require substantial reductions in basic cable rates. Rapid changes in technology, including the development of direct broadcast satellites and cellular cable, and even initial telephone company investments in broadband capacity could also have been responsible for part or all of the decline. We return to this matter in chapter 4.

It is surprising that neither the FCC nor Congress mentioned another key finding of the 1990 GAO followup report—that ShowTime rates fell in nominal terms in 1986–89, while HBO and Cinemax remained about the same.[35] This occurred even though the quality of services had improved and real incomes had risen throughout the period. Apparently, cable operators had so increased the number and quality of basic services that prices

---

must cover a substantial single geographic area. If they have a large number of noncontiguous franchises in a metropolitan area, they will have much more difficulty offering such services.

34. If the act actually unleashed monopoly power, one would have to argue that the market did not recognize the situation for three years, then belatedly began to reflect the industry's new market power. We do not find such an explanation persuasive.

35. General Accounting Office, *Follow-Up National Survey*, table III.2.

for the premium services had to be reined in. The concurrent proliferation of video cassette recorders surely provides another explanation. However, had cable operators been extracting monopoly charges by raising the relative price of basic service and restricting output, the price of the premium channel alternatives would more likely have risen.

Of course, it is possible that cable operators did not have much market power before deregulation but that their power increased in the late 1980s. As long as they could offer little beyond the retransmission of broadcast signals, consumers might have been willing to discontinue service if prices increased too much. After 1984, however, as technology allowed systems to carry more channels and systems filled the capability with better programming from cable networks rather than with retransmitted broadcast signals, market power may have increased. This could be part of the explanation for rising basic cable rates after 1986.

Regulating the Cable "Monopoly"

Even if cable operations have market power in many places across the country, should rates be regulated, and how? Designing an efficient regulatory pricing scheme for even the simplest, undifferentiated "natural-monopoly" services such as supplying natural gas or water, is far from easy.[36] For a dynamic industry with rapidly changing technology, highly differentiated products, and rapid obsolescence for most of its capital structure and service offerings, regulation is far more complicated and has the potential to induce major reductions in service quality.

The traditional problems in regulating natural monopolies derive from the existence of asymmetric information and the need to preserve incentives for efficiency, ensure minimum levels of quality, and measure important parameters. Asymmetric information occurs because a regulated company has better access to information on costs and demand than do its regulators. This asymmetry is not easily overcome, particularly in an industry with rapid technical change and heterogeneous products.

Incentives for efficiency are invariably reduced when regulators confine the regulated company to a maximum rate of return or maximum level of

36. There is a very large literature on optimal regulation. See, for example, Kenneth Train, *Optimal Regulation: The Economic Theory of Natural Monopoly* (MIT Press, 1991). For the direct application of this literature to telecommunications, see Bridger M. Mitchell and Ingo Vogelsang, *Telecommunications Pricing: Theory and Practice* (Cambridge University Press, 1991).

profit. The most common solution for this problem is to use rate caps to limit price increases to the rate of inflation less an offset for expected productivity gains greater than the average for the economy. Such price regulation is compromised, however, by regulators' periodic reviews of the regulated firm's profitability and the difficulty of accommodating new services under the cap.[37]

In every regulatory regime a constrained monopolist may be able to respond to regulation by reducing the quality of its service and therefore its costs at the regulated price. Under traditional rate-of-return regulation, such behavior would result in excessive profits that, in turn, would have to be reduced by a future rate cut. Under rate caps, no such palliative is available, so regulators are even more concerned about service quality.

All regulatory regimes are also hostage to difficulties in measuring important parameters. Under traditional rate-of-return regulation, the most difficult problem is to estimate the cost of capital. For rate caps the problem is to estimate the expected rate of productivity growth. For regulatory regimes that attempt to control all of the rates of a multiservice company, not just their average levels, the problems are even more severe because regulators must have information on incremental costs and demand elasticities for each service.

All the difficulties of traditional rate regulation are magnified with the cable television industry. The nature of the service, the technology for delivering it, and consumer demand are constantly changing. Systems that were once able to offer only twelve channels can now provide fifty or more. Premium channels devoted to sports, movies, and live entertainment were added in the 1970s to augment the offerings of distant broadcast signals. Pay-per-view channels were added to augment the premium channels. Most recently, business news and home shopping channels have been developed to fill the growing technical capacity of cable systems. In each case, program quality varies enormously but is difficult to measure.

If each of the more than 11,000 cable systems in the United States offered subscribers only one tier of programming with identical networks, the task of regulation would be much simpler. Although the mechanics of calculating the regulated rate would still be far from trivial, the rate could be applied to every system in the country. But cable systems, of course, do not offer uniform programming; each offers a different mix of cable networks, broadcast stations, local programs, billboards, and other services. Many offer more than one tier of programming. And each system

---

37. For a discussion of rate caps, see the symposium in *RAND Journal of Economics*, vol. 20 (Autumn 1989), pp. 369–472.

offers rentals of converters, remote controls, and other equipment and services that are also covered by the 1992 Cable Act. The result requires complicated calculations to determine the regulated rates for each system.

This is only the beginning of the problem. Systems are now being positioned and even reconfigured to deliver switched, or interactive, services, including voice, data, and information services. Meanwhile, telephone networks are being rebuilt to allow them to deliver video services. In both cases the costs of any one service are often joint and common costs. There is no easy way for regulators to allocate them nor to determine the fairness of rates offered in a competitive market by a company with regulated monopoly services delivered under these conditions.[38]

The imposition of rate-of-return or price regulations on cable television requires that the regulator first specify the quality of each regulated service. If there is to be basic service and a premium service, what differentiates them? Regulators may decree that off-air broadcast signals plus a local government channel, Cable News Network, and CSPAN constitute basic service, while all other channels, except those focusing exclusively on movies or sports are in an enhanced basic or cable programming tier. But what if CNN splits into two services after regulation is imposed, offering different services on each? Or what if an erstwhile enhanced basic channel upgrades its programming and requires that cable operators offer it as a premium channel? And if regulation reduces the willingness of cable operators to pay for a national satellite-delivered service, how will the regulator know if this leads to a reduction in programming quality?

Finally, if rate-of-return regulation is employed, how do regulators determine the cost of programming, particularly if the cable systems hold different levels of equity in their various program services? Even if these intangible programming costs could be estimated with any precision, enormous regulatory problems remain because cable systems will have the incentive to alter the quality of the service under a given rate constraint.

Regulation before 1984

The 1984 Cable Act is often thought of as a deregulatory statute like the Airline Deregulation Act of 1978 or similar laws that deregulated oil

38. The standard approach to this problem is to place a floor under the competitive rates based on the incremental cost of service. See, for example, William J. Baumol and J. Gregory Sidak, *Toward Competition in Local Telephony* (MIT Press and the American Enterprise Institute, 1994). This approach is, however, fraught with problems because firms may choose a technology in which the attributable incremental costs of the competitive service are close to zero even if the technology is more expensive than others that generate

prices, natural gas prices, air cargo rates, or trucking rates. But cable rates were not regulated in the same manner as those for other goods or services. Cable systems were generally franchised by municipal authorities who did not usually follow any formal regulatory process, especially not cost-of-service regulation. Some state regulatory agencies exercised control over cable rates, but otherwise operators were subject to less formal scrutiny under the terms of their franchise agreement.

Municipal regulation often focused on a cable operator's promise to pay a franchise fee or tax, partly as compensation for the use of public rights of way, and to offer subsidized or free service to local governmental or civic institutions. Most franchise agreements specified the services subscribers would be offered and the rates they were to be charged, as well as various rate-adjustment mechanisms. Enforcement of the contracts sometimes resulted in vigorous disputes, but few studies have examined how much municipal rate restraints were actually binding.[39] As the result of court decisions, municipalities could not control the content of cable programming, and they rarely intervened in decisions regarding the extent of the service—the number of channels, for example—a local operator chose to offer. In fact, many cable companies thought of themselves as essentially unregulated even before the 1984 act took effect.

In its 1992 survey the Federal Communications Commission asked each cable system whether it was subject to rate regulation as of November 30, 1986. We analyzed a sample of the responses and found that the systems that were regulated in 1986 charged average basic rates of $13.39 a month (in 1992 dollars) and those that were not regulated charged $15.88. After accounting for differences in service levels, the differences in basic rates are not statistically significant. The programming changes instituted by these systems between 1986 and 1992 were, however, statistically significant, suggesting that regulation may have impaired cable service quality if not cable rates.[40]

---

much higher incremental costs.

39. An exception is Mark A. Zupan, "The Efficacy of Franchise Bidding Schemes in the Case of Cable Television: Some Systematic Evidence," *Journal of Law and Economics,* vol. 32 (October 1989), pp. 401–56. Zupan concluded that competitive bidding for franchises was successful in reducing cable rates before passage of the 1984 Cable Act but was not completely successful in eliminating monopoly rents.

40. Of a sample of 146 systems providing complete data, 65 reported they were regulated in 1986. For analysis see chapter 3.

The 1992 Cable Act

Federal, state, and local governments have regulated the conduct of some industries for decades, and the division of responsibility has been fairly stable. Utilities providing local services are regulated by local and state authorities. Those providing interstate services—oil pipelines or long-distance telephone companies—are regulated by federal authorities. But federal economic regulation began to wane in the late 1970s. Indeed, between the 1930s and 1992 the only lasting new federal industry-specific program of price regulation was the Federal Power Commission's regulation of the natural gas industry, which began in the 1950s.[41] The resuscitation of cable television rate regulation by the 1992 Cable Act was thus a major departure from trends of the previous twenty-five years. The return to regulation was ostensibly intended to prevent the cable industry from exploiting the pricing power Congress believed had been uncovered by the GAO reports of 1989 and 1990.

Major Provisions

In passing the 1992 act, Congress was determined to do far more than establish federal regulation of cable subscribers' monthly rates. The act instituted extensive federal and state regulation of services that was to be coordinated by the FCC. Of its twenty-six sections, only one specifically addressed cable rates. Others authorized federal regulation of the carriage of commercial and noncommercial stations, retransmission consent, consumer protection and customer service, leased commercial access, itemization of customer bills, protection of children from indecent programming, consumer notification of sexually explicit programming, and technical standards and signal quality. The act placed federal restrictions on cable operator ownership of other forms of video distribution and on contractual terms between cable operators and programming distributors, terms for the sale of cable systems, and terms for services from direct broadcast satellite carriers. It also required the FCC to improve the compatibility of consumer electronics equipment, develop competition and diversity in video programming and distribution, and promote equal employment opportunities.

---

41. Other examples of federal efforts to regulate prices—in the airlines, trucking, oil, and natural gas industries—were ended in the 1970s and 1980s after price regulation was discovered to be unambiguously harmful.

Even if the 1992 Cable Act had not authorized rate regulation, the other provisions would have had important effects on cable operators and consumers. Conforming with them entails new compliance costs and costs of lost business opportunities. Moreover, the rules may be partly responsible for the large MSOs' continuing acquisitions of smaller operators, because large operators can spread the fixed costs of compliance among a larger group of subscribers.

The most visible and perhaps most important provisions, however, are those governing the regulation of cable rates. The act defines basic service and equipment services and authorizes their regulation based on an "effective competition" standard; it also authorizes regulation of other cable programming services, such as other packages of basic service, on a "reasonableness" standard (which the FCC is to decide).[42] HBO, Showtime, and other premium channels are not regulated, nor are à la carte, nonpremium channels that are offered individually to subscribers. However, cable operators may not shift program services among tiers or between cable programming and à la carte services to avoid rate regulation. Given the complexity of the act's provisions for rate regulation, it is not surprising that litigation has focused heavily on them.[43]

The act defines effective competition in a way that represents a sharp departure from conventional economic approaches to measuring it. Effective competition is assumed to exist if one of three circumstances exists:

(A) fewer than 30 percent of the households in the franchise area subscribe to the cable service of a cable system;

(B) the franchise area is (i) served by at least two unaffiliated multichannel video programming distributors each of which offers comparable video programming to at least 50 percent of the households in the franchise area; and (ii) the number of households subscribing to programming services offered by multichannel video programming distributors other than the largest multichannel video programming distributor exceeds 15 percent of the households in the franchise area; or

(C) operated by a multichannel video programming distributor, the franchising authority for that franchise area offers video programming to at least 50 percent of the households in the franchise area.[44]

Franchises that fail to meet one of these criteria are subject to the full burden of rate regulation.

---

42. 47 U.S.C. §543(a), (b), and (c).
43. See, for example, 56 F.3d 151 (D.C. Cir. 1995).
44. 47 U.S.C.543(l).

Promulgation of Regulations

The FCC was responsible for writing de novo regulations for all sections of the act, and did so under very tight deadlines, a heroic and unenviable task. One of the first responsibilities was to measure the effect of competition. In carrying out this task, the commission canvassed 748 cable systems for data on rates, service offerings, and competition as of October 1992. These systems were drawn from a 500-system random sample and 248 that were chosen because they seemed to meet one of the three criteria for effective competition. From the 687 complete, unduplicated responses it received, the commission found that it had data on 1,107 separate community operations, since some systems operate in more than one community that has independent franchising authority. Of the 1,107 operations, 79 seemed to face competition as defined under the first criterion (less than 30 percent penetration), 46 under the second (two or more competing systems), and 16 under the third (municipal-owned system). These 145 units provided the basis for the FCC to determine by regression analysis the benchmark rates for competitive markets. The initial regression analysis concluded that rates were 9.4 percent lower in competitive than in non-competitive franchise areas.[45]

Like most laws that authorize government agencies to regulate, the Cable Act of 1992 used broad and flexible language. It left most of the details of regulation to the FCC. Within that framework, the commission chose to use the effective competition standard for all tiers of service, not just basic cable packages. By discarding a separate reasonableness standard, it placed enormous weight on its survey of cable operators and the statistical analysis of the survey results.

---

45. Rates were actually regulated revenues per subscriber. This measure included equipment rentals, installations, and fees for basic service; see 8 FCC Rcd 5631 (1993). The regression model estimated was unusual. It related price charged per channel of nonpremium service to the number of channels offered, the number of satellite-delivered (basic cable) networks, and the reciprocal of system subscribers. It reported results that price per channel falls with increases in the number of channels, but rises with the number of satellite-delivered channels and with the reciprocal of system size (subscribers). It is difficult to understand why system size per se should affect price unless the economies of scale are important among the small systems that the FCC sampled rather heavily. Alternatively, system size may be serving as a proxy for density or for a later franchise date that locks in a higher rate in an inflationary era. Moreover, it is difficult to understand why the price per channel should increase as the number of basic cable networks increases. It is more likely that the FCC uncovered a different phenomenon: that cable systems offer more basic service channels in markets where the demand for cable is high, not that, all else equal, the value of these signals to consumers rises as their number increases.

At first, the FCC announced that cable rates would be regulated based on the benchmark price regression.[46] Franchises with rates more than 10 percent higher than the benchmark rate would be required to reduce average regulated revenue by 10 percent. Franchises with rates less than 10 percent higher than the benchmark had to reduce them to the benchmark. Franchises with rates at or below the benchmark were not required to reduce rates. Separately, equipment rental rates were required to reflect costs. The net effect was to reduce equipment rental rates in many franchises.

The FCC predicted that basic rates would decline by about 10 percent under this standard.[47] Cable systems could petition for cost-of-service reviews of the adequacy of the rates once the commission had established guidelines for the reviews. But even before the benchmarks were implemented, controversy erupted over the size of the rollback they would engender. After several months the FCC decided to review the entire matter. An analysis of changes in cable rates between April 1, 1993, and September 1, 1993 (the effective date of the new regulations), for the largest MSOs found that average revenue from regulated service had fallen by 6 percent and that much of this decline had come from reductions in rental rates on equipment.[48]

The act allowed just 180 days for issuing rate regulations but set no limitation on the number of times the commission could revise them.[49] Nor did it attempt to limit the complexity of the regulations. Confusion and uncertainty were bound to ensue among cable operators and consumers alike.

Under pressure from Congress and consumer groups that the initial reductions were inadequate, the FCC announced in February 1994 a further 7 percent rollback in basic rates, thus implying that it had effected a 17 percent reduction under the benchmark.[50] The 1994 rules established a new benchmark based on another regression analysis, which differed from the 1993 study in that it used different variables and accounted separately

46. 8 FCC Rcd 5631 (1993).
47. 8 FCC Rcd 5631 (1993).
48. Federal Communications Commission, Cable Services Bureau, "FCC Regulation Impact Survey Changes in Cable Television Rates between April 5, 1993, and September 1, 1993: Report and Summary," February 22, 1994. Rental rates on equipment are based on system costs plus a reasonable profit.
49. 47 U.S.C. § 543 (b) and (c).
50. 9 FCC Rcd 4119 (1994). For all franchises not subject to effective competition, rates were eventually to fall by 17 percent relative to their September 30, 1992, levels, regardless of the relationship between existing rates and the benchmark.

for the influence of each of the three categories of presumably competitive situations. In 1993 when all three situations were combined into one dichotomous "competitive" variable, the FCC staff found that competition reduced rates 9.4 percent below those in noncompetitive situations. In 1994 it was asserting that the figure should be 17 percent.

In 1993 and 1994 the FCC staff found that, when it combined situations in which there was municipal ownership and competition into one dichotomous dummy variable reflecting competition, rates were 28 percent lower than in other markets. There was some pressure within the agency to set a benchmark that could be announced as rolling rates back 28 percent. But the 1994 regression equation, using separate variables for each of the three competitive situations, indicated no significant rate difference in areas of low penetration, a 37 percent lower rate for areas with municipal systems, and a 16 percent lower rate for overbuilt markets compared with markets in which none of these conditions existed. As a result, the commission was able to reach a "reasonable" compromise for a 17 percent rollback.

The compromise was achieved at a high cost in FCC credibility. Not only had the commission appeared to manipulate its empirical analysis to accommodate political pressure, but it was forced to publish a regression it claimed was "too complicated" for cable system owners to understand.[51] These operators, presumably lacking access to calculators or personal computers, would probably have to ask the highly skilled FCC staff to estimate the benchmark for them. In fact, when finally released, the regression results were embarrassing.

First, cable systems owned by large MSOs were allowed under the transitional rules to charge substantially more for the same service than were locally owned systems.[52] A system with 10,000 subscribers that offered fifty channels, forty of them devoted to basic cable networks, had a 1994 benchmark of $16.40 a month if it were owned by the largest cable company in the country. If the system were independently owned, it would be allowed to charge no more than $13.88 (table 2-2).

---

51. Indeed, the FCC approved the *Second Order* on February 22, 1994, but did not release it until March 30, an unusually long delay for the commission.

52. Although cable systems not meeting the effective-competition standard were required eventually to reduce rates by the full 17 percent relative to September 1992 levels, franchises would have to reduce rates only down to the benchmark if that reduction were less than 17 percent. Under the transitional rules, however, cable operators could not raise rates with inflation until real rates were lower than the September 1992 levels. See 9 FCC Rcd 4119 (1994), sections 106–113.

Table 2-2. *FCC Basic-Package Benchmark Rates for Cable Systems with 10,000 Subscribers or More, 1994*

System characteristics	System				
	A	B	C	D	E
Channel capacity	50	50	50	500	500
Basic cable networks	40	40	40	490	490
Multiple system owner	Yes	Yes	No	Yes	No
Size of MSO (millions of subscribers)	10	1	...	10	...
Benchmark rate (dollars per month)	16.40	16.24	13.88	17.62	14.91

Source: Authors' calculations.

Second, even if the independent system had expanded to 500 channels in 1994 with 490 channels of basic service, it would have been allowed to charge just $14.91 a month, or less than the MSO operating a 50-channel system.[53] A tenfold difference in output would have been rewarded by a revenue loss of $12.00 a year for each subscriber.[54] Table 2-2 also shows that greater cable capacity generated a higher benchmark for a large MSO than did the same capacity for the independent system, but neither would likely have been better off carrying 500 channels to get just $12.00 or $14.00 more in subscriber revenues each year.

Third, the initial FCC rules for future activities—so-called going-forward rules—offered most cable operators only a penny per channel per month for a typical expansion of basic service.[55] Cable operators would have had little incentive to expand basic service, and program suppliers would have had no market for their new networks. In late 1994 the commission amended the rules to give cable operators some incentive to add channels to regulated service tiers. The amended rules backed away from strict price regulation for new service. Rates charged for additional channels that formed a new tier of service would be subject to less stringent regulation than rates for existing cable programming. Rates for à la carte channels would not be regulated as long as the services were not simply transparent attempts to avoid rate regulation on existing tiers of service.[56]

---

53. Five hundred channels is a widely discussed possibility, given the digital compression technologies now available.

54. These rules applied to the service offerings in effect as of August 1994. Different rules would govern new services.

55. 7 FCC Rcd 5781 (1992).

56. 10 FCC Rcd 1226 (1995).

Fourth, the FCC's benchmark estimate of competitive cable rates disintegrates when franchises outside metropolitan statistical areas (MSAs) are excluded from the regression analysis. The results of both the 1993 and 1994 analyses were heavily influenced by the large number of small, rural franchises in the sample. Competition among franchises in MSAs that now represent the vast majority of all subscribers does not reduce rates for basic service. The same was true when the FCC's regression analysis applied only to those systems with more than 5,000 subscribers.[57] Direct competition from more than one system appears to reduce cable rates only in rural areas. Presumably, other market forces discipline cable rates in urban and suburban areas such that system operators cannot significantly raise rates.

The benchmarks were only the beginning of the 1992 Cable Act's regulatory requirements. The 1994 rules also specified a cap for determining rates in subsequent years.[58] A pass-through equal to the rate of inflation less an offset for increased productivity is allowed only for those costs not considered exogenous, but exogenous costs include programming costs, taxes, franchise fees, copyright fees, and the like. And programming costs cannot simply be the fee charged by cable networks if the cable system has an equity interest of 5 percent or more in the network and if 25 percent or more of the network's subscribers are on systems with this 5 percent (or greater) equity interest.

The FCC has also issued rules charging municipal franchising authorities with the responsibility of determining the cost of basic services when a review is requested and of setting maximum charges on pay-per-view telecasts of championship events in major sports. Other regulations govern the allowable extent of vertical integration into programming and require carriage of local broadcast signals, maintenance of minimum technical standards, equipment compatibility between television sets and new technologies, the assurance of continued sports programming, equal employment opportunity, and public-interest programming for direct broadcast satellites. Given 11,000 cable systems and perhaps 30,000 franchising authorities, the scope and complexity of this new regulatory regime could be staggering.

---

57. Most cable franchises have fewer than 5,000 subscribers and together serve only 13 percent of U.S. subscribers. The FCC acknowledged this but nevertheless adopted the rules based on the regression model for all systems. See 7 FCC Rcd 5781 (1992), app. C, pp. 22–24.

58. These rules are curiously called "spring forward" rate adjustments.

Incentive Effects

It is possible that the regulation of basic and other programming services would have only minor effects on industry efficiency because they are not at the frontier of cable development. Reducing cash flows from them is not likely to cause cable systems to reduce their quality or quantity if the systems are fully built, but it could affect the companies' ability to generate resources to invest in new services. In addition, the 1992 act provides for the possibility of some regulation of pay-per-view offerings, suggesting that Congress was not entirely opposed to the regulation of new industry developments, such as switched interactive services.[59]

Not all cable programming services are regulated by the 1992 act. Premium networks and à la carte channels are still largely unregulated. The incentives to shift channels from regulated basic service to unregulated services are substantial. Just how the cable rules operate to prevent this in an environment in which there is substantial turnover of networks and formats and how cable operators will avoid the worst effects of regulation remains to be seen.

Uncertainty and the Changing Face of Regulation

By altering the structure of cable rate regulation between 1993 and 1994, the FCC demonstrated the impermanence of the initial regulatory architecture and possibly any future form. The 1994 regulations established not only a precedent for replacing one structure with another but a precedent for doing so in response to public pressure.

For cable industry investors, any form of rate regulation is bad, and unpredictable regulation is worse. If today's allowed rate may be disallowed tomorrow, the uncertainty increases the risk of doing business in the industry and investment may flee toward more solid prospects.

The FCC has continued to promulgate new rules in its effort to implement the act. In late 1994, for example, it developed rate regulations that would allow cable operators to recover as much as 20 cents per subscriber per month for each channel added to an existing tier of service, but in no case could regulated rates increase by more than a total of $1.40 per subscriber between January 1, 1995, and December 31, 1997. Separately, cable operators may offer new channels à la carte or bundled as a tier virtually

---

59. The act and the FCC's implementation of it were blamed for the collapse of the Bell Atlantic–TCI merger in February 1994.

free of regulation.[60] Mercifully, some of the regulated cable rates will now expire in 1999.

Regulating the Competitors

A potentially more serious problem than the short-term effects of rate changes is the dampening effect of a broad and unpredictable regulatory program on the development of new services or technologies. The 1992 act specifically allows for rate regulation of certain pay-per-view services and places signal-carriage obligations—requirements for carrying public-interest programming—on an expensive and risky technology, direct broadcast satellites. The act's concern with everything from program ownership to DBS services was not very encouraging to adventuresome telecommunications companies. In 1984 Congress deregulated cable television, freeing operators to develop new services that became candidates for regulation just eight years later.[61] Now, just a few years later, Congress has once again moved to deregulate cable rates, although this deregulation does not become fully effective until 1999.

Telephone Company Competition

For decades, regulators have been concerned with both the potential for telephone companies to abuse their franchised monopoly positions to enter other communications markets and the potential for competition in telephony posed by cable. In 1970 the FCC barred all telephone common carriers from providing cable television service in their own franchise areas.[62] (Some waivers from this ban were granted, however, and by 1990 about 300 of the country's 8,400 cable systems were owned by telephone companies.)[63] This ban was codified in the 1984 Cable Act. Congress thus deregulated cable rates at the same time it formally insulated cable companies from competition. In 1993, however, Bell Atlantic challenged the constitutionality of the ban in a federal appeals court and won.[64] Before the 1996

60. A la carte channels cannot have migrated from a regulated tier of service. See 10 FCC Rcd 1226 (1995).

61. To its credit, the FCC claimed to be searching for a way to limit its rate regulation to just basic service. The 1996 act requires it to do so.

62. 22 FCC 2d 746 (1970).

63. Michael K. Kellogg, John Thorne, and Peter W. Huber, *Federal Telecommunications Law* (Boston: Little, Brown, 1992), p. 700.

64. *The Chesapeake and Potomac Telephone Company of Virginia v. United States,* 830 F.Supp. 909 (E.D. Va. 1993), *aff'd,* 42 F3d 181 (4th cir. 1994) *cert granted.*

act the FCC had permitted telephone companies to offer video dial tone in their franchise areas on a leased basis to outside programmers, but it had limited the companies' interests in programming ventures to just 5 percent.[65] These restrictions stemmed from a fear that regulated telephone monopolists might attempt to subsidize new video (or any other competitive) services by diverting the development costs into the cost accounts of their regulated enterprises.

There is some debate as to the feasibility of telephone company competition in video services. Leland Johnson has argued that telephone companies are unlikely to undertake the large investment required to adapt their networks to deliver video unless they can offer services different from those offered by cable systems.[66] Still, Pacific Bell proposed to rebuild its entire California network at a cost of $16 billion, extending a fiber optics/coaxial cable system so it can provide broadband and narrowband services over the same lines. The proposal has stirred considerable controversy because Pacific Bell argues that the incremental cost for the video dial tone capacity is only $136 per home passed.[67] Critics contend that the full cost of the network could be more than $2,500 per home, of which far more than $136 is properly attributable to video services. By contrast, New Jersey Bell filed a more limited proposal to build a fiber optics/coaxial cable system in New Jersey whose incremental video dial tone investment was estimated at $459 to $491 per home.[68] This proposal has now been abandoned in favor of a "fiber-to-the-curb" architecture, and Pacific Bell has also slowed its construction of the new network.[69]

Obviously, regulators will find it difficult to estimate precisely the incremental costs of various regulated services. They may, however, be able to negotiate regulatory compacts in which conventional telephone rates are controlled by a rate cap, video services are tariffed but essentially unregulated, and the carrier assumes full responsibility for all investment in advanced technology.

---

65. 7 FCC Rcd 5781, 5789 (1992). These rules are largely moot in the wake of the 1996 act.

66. Leland L. Johnson, *Toward Competition in Cable Television* (MIT Press and the American Enterprise Institute, 1994).

67. Federal Communications Commission, "In the Matter of the Application of Pacific Bell. . .," file no. W-P-C 6913-16, "Affidavit of Leland L. Johnson" (1993), and "Declaration of Robert G. Harris" (1994).

68. See "Affidavit of Leland Johnson."

69. The status of these programs at the end of 1995 is summarized in Barry Phillips, "Video Technologies Seek Title Bout," *Telephony,* vol. 229 (November 6, 1995), pp. 36–43.

Direct Broadcast Satellites

In 1994 two direct broadcast satellite operations were launched. Each requires the subscriber to obtain a moderate-sized receiver that costs about $700 plus installation. These systems are not operated in conjunction with any regulated service; they involve no public rights of way. They will be competing with cable television, traditional broadcasting, prospective telephone company video services, and (arguably) even video cassette rentals. In short, there is no case for public regulation of their services.[70]

Nevertheless, regulation of DBS was mandated by Congress. The 1992 Cable Act required that between 4 and 7 percent of DBS channels be reserved for "noncommercial programming of an educational or informational nature." These channels were to be made available to "national educational programming suppliers" at "reasonable" rates, that is, at rates not to exceed 50 percent of "the total direct costs of making such channels available."[71] The act was silent on how such direct costs were to be determined when most costs of a DBS service would be common costs for all channels. More troubling, however, was the lack of a rationale for imposing the requirements. Clearly, DBS systems would enjoy little or no market power. Why, then, did Congress feel that handicapping them with noncompensatory carriage requirements was in the public interest? Fortunately, the courts have invalidated these requirements.[72]

The Telecommunications Act of 1996

The Telecommunications Act of 1996 advances competition for cable television systems and removes some of the rate regulation established by the 1992 act. The 1984 ban on telephone company provision of cable service in its own territory is eliminated, as is the requirement that all video service platforms be approved by the FCC under section 214. Telephone companies may now invest in cable programming and do not have to operate as video common carriers.

---

70. Someone must allocate the frequencies and orbital slots for the geostationary satellites, but a market could easily do so. Even with FCC allocation of these scarce property rights, however, there is no economic reason for regulating the content, the number of channels, or the rates charged to subscribers.

71. *Cable Television Consumer Protection and Competition Act of 1992*, sec. 335 (b)(1), (3), (4)(B).

72. *Daniels Cablevision v. FCC,* 835 F. Supp. 1 (D.C. Cir., 1993).

The 1996 act removes rate regulation for all but the basic tier of cable services. Deregulation occurs immediately for rural areas even though rural cable systems are more likely to enjoy market power than are urban ones. The effect of "competition," as defined in the 1992 act, on rates was discernable only in nonurban areas. In urban areas, deregulation of nonbasic tiers of service becomes effective only when competition exists or when a telephone company launches its entry into broadband services. Otherwise, such regulation remains until 1999.

The entire federal regulatory superstructure remains, as do all of the other nonprice provisions of the 1992 act. Thus a future Congress could easily reintroduce full rate regulation without the necessity of rebuilding a regulatory staff at the FCC. The path is clear for yet another political course reversal.

Conclusion

We are profoundly skeptical that regulation can be employed to increase consumer welfare. Even if cable companies have market power, attempts to set rates for diverse services are likely to be arbitrary. As such they will become a reason to skimp on quality and will eventually be avoided or evaded. The exemptions for premium and à la carte services could eventually be eliminated, which would likely further reduce incentives for developing new programming services. As cable technology gravitates from the capability of delivering 50 or more channels to perhaps delivering 500, it would be particularly unfortunate if operators had little motivation to fill these channels with attractive material. Fortunately, in 1996 Congress again changed course.

Just two years after the passage of the 1992 Cable Act, the Democrats lost their majority status in both houses of Congress. Almost immediately, new proposals on telecommunications regulation emerged from both chambers. The Republican Congress has now rolled back most of the provisions of the act that require rate regulation. Unfortunately, no one has yet provided analyses of the welfare effects of the 1986–92 deregulation of cable, much less those of the 1992–96 reregulation. Therefore, we next address the deregulation that followed in the wake of the 1984 act. This analysis should provide an estimate of the effects of a more modest regime of rate regulation administered in a generally ad hoc fashion by many municipal and state authorities. A preliminary analysis of the effects of the 1992–96 regime of reregulation is reported in chapter 4.

CHAPTER THREE

Effects on Consumers of Changes in Cable Service

T HE Cable Television Consumer Protection and Competition Act of 1992 was created in large part as a response to the rate increases that followed deregulation. A 1990 General Accounting Office report simply confirmed what most people already knew: cable rates had risen much faster than inflation after deregulation became effective in 1986.[1] Unfortunately, no one asked whether cable subscribers were better off in 1990 or 1992 than they had been in 1986. Or, alternatively, were they better off in 1992 than they would have been if regulation had continued? Had these questions been asked, the answers might have relieved much of the pressure for the reregulation of the industry in 1990–92.

Consumer Demand for Cable Service

Any analysis of the effects of cable industry regulation on economic welfare must include some model of consumer demand. Such models should include the determinants of cable subscription: the prices and qualities of various service options, the prices of substitutes, the consumer's income, and a variety of other demographic variables that might reasonably affect the probability of choosing to subscribe.

There are essentially two approaches to estimating the demand for cable television. The first and more common involves estimating cable systems' subscriber penetration, that is, the ratio of subscribers to the number of homes the system passes.[2] Unfortunately, studies using this approach are filled with problems because they attempt to match average demographic characteristics and incomes for some geographic or political jurisdiction

---

1. General Accounting Office, *Follow-up National Survey of Cable Television Rates and Services,* GAO/RCED 90-199 (June 1990).

2. See appendix A for a much more detailed discussion of this matter.

with average demand for cable services offered by a system that is rarely coterminous with that jurisdiction. Moreover, they often suffer from an identification (or causation) problem: Is penetration low because prices are high or are prices set in some political or economic fashion in response to perceptions of consumer demand?

A far better approach to estimating the demand for cable services is to specify a model of the probability of household subscription and to estimate it using household data. Such a method greatly reduces identification problems and errors in variables, but it is difficult to undertake because of the lack of public data on household characteristics such as cable television subscription and the identity of the local cable system. We overcame these problems by contracting through a consumer survey organization for a 1992 national survey of approximately 750 randomly drawn households.[3] Using these data and information on each household's location, we have collected public data on the relevant cable systems for 1983–84 and 1992 to estimate a logit demand model and the changes in economic welfare attributable to changes in cable rates and services between 1984 and 1992.

A Multinomial Logit Model of the Demand for Cable Service

In appendix B we derive a multinomial logit model that expresses the probability of a household's selecting any one of three options: subscribing only to basic cable services, subscribing to basic and premium services, or not subscribing.[4] This model includes as explanatory variables the monthly fee for basic service (*PRICE*),[5] the monthly fee for basic service plus one premium channel (*PREMP*),[6] the number of basic satellite-delivered networks

---

3. The details of the survey methodology and the resulting data set are described in appendix B. To the extent that the sample is representative of U.S. households, the parameter estimates and welfare calculations based on it are estimates that are valid for the population of U.S. households.

4. The validity of the multinomial logit specification turns importantly on satisfying the condition of the independence of irrelevant alternatives (IIA). We show in appendix B that our model satisfies this condition.

5. By *basic service* we refer to the standard package of programming services, excluding premium services, offered by cable operators in 1992. In the 1992 act these services are referred to as the combination of basic service and cable programming service, which includes all nonpremium services. At the time of our survey these distinctions were unknown; subscribers to systems with more than one tier of basic service usually subscribed to all tiers.

6. Wherever it is available, we use the rate for HBO as the rate for premium channels.

on the system ($BASAT$),[7] the number of premium services ($PREM$),[8] the number of off-air (broadcast) stations provided by the system ($OFFAIR$), the number of nonduplicated stations available to the household without cable ($NONDUP$),[9] the logarithm of the cable system's age ($LSYSAGE$), the household's monthly income (Y), a dummy variable for rural residence ($RURA$), a dummy variable for a household head 65 years of age or older ($AGE65$), a dummy variable equal to one if the household has been at its present address for five or more years ($TIME5$), a dummy variable equal to one if the household is a single person ($FSIZE1$), and a dummy variable indicating VCR ownership. Complete data were obtained for 441 households. The sample distribution of each variable is shown in appendix table B-1.

The parameter estimates and associated t-statistics for the multinomial logit model are shown in table 3-1.[10] The table provides the parameter estimates for the choice to subscribe only to basic cable services and the estimates for the choice to subscribe to both basic and premium services. The sensitivity of the third choice, no cable subscription, to the economic variables can be inferred from the parameters for these other two choices.

Changes in Consumer Welfare

We used the results of our multinomial logit model to estimate the effects on consumer welfare of changes in service characteristics or cable rates.[11] For this purpose we calculated the compensating variation that one would have to pay (or receive from) a consumer after any change in prices or ser-

7. The most important of these networks as of late 1993 are shown in table 1-3. They include CNN, ESPN, The Learning Channel, and other networks that are offered in various basic or expanded basic packages for a fixed monthly price.

8. These are the premium networks such as HBO and Showtime that are offered individually or bundled with other similar services for a fixed monthly fee. See table 1-3 for a list of the most important.

9. This is the number of broadcast television signals available in the household's ZIP code. We used the industry's B-contour standard of reception. We define *nonduplicated* as those broadcast stations that do not offer essentially the same programming as others that can be received off the air in that market. For example, a second CBS or ABC network affiliate in a viewing area would be a duplicate network station and thus would not be counted.

10. The equation is B.15 in appendix B.

11. For a review of these techniques, see John S. Chipman and James C. Moore, "Compensating Variation, Consumer's Surplus, and Welfare," *American Economic Review*, vol. 70 (December 1980), pp. 933–49.

Table 3-1. *Estimated Parameters for Multinomial Logit Model*[a]

Basic-only equation		Basic-plus-premium equation	
Variable	Statistic	Variable	Statistic
CONSTANT	−2.75290**	CONSTANT	−1.5583
	(−2.457)		(−1.116)
PRICE	−0.4750***	PREMP	−0.04750***
	(−5.993)		(−5.993)
BASAT	−0.04843**	BASAT	−0.04958**
	(2.146)		(2.256)
		PREM	−0.04573
			(−0.827)
OFFAIR	0.07208	OFFAIR	0.05419
	(1.369)		(0.835)
NONDUP	−0.10503**	NONDUP	−0.04447
	(−1.998)		(−0.744)
RURA	−0.24028	RURA	−1.03592*
	(−0.741)		(−1.673)
LSYSAGE	1.00492***	LSYSAGE	0.47845
	(3.374)		(1.508)
Y	0.00004	Y	0.00010
	(0.536)		(1.312)
AGE65	1.06534***	AGE65	0.25173
	(3.564)		(0.450)
TIME5	−0.63397**	TIME5	−0.26304
	(−2.553)		(−0.805)
FSIZE1	−0.18733	FSIZE1	−0.59924
	(−0.658)		(−1.475)
VCR	0.37156***	VCR	0.83238**
	(8.621)		(2.230)

Source: Authors' calculations.
a. Degrees of freedom, 417; log of the likelihood function, −441.850. Asymptotic *t*-statistics are in parentheses.
* Significantly different from zero at 10 percent confidence interval.
** Significantly different from zero at 5 percent confidence interval.
*** Significantly different from zero at 1 percent confidence interval.

vice levels or both to make the consumer as well off as he or she was in the initial condition.[12] Because our demand model was based on 1992 values, we estimated the compensating variation, or how much a household would have to be paid or to pay to be as well off under various cable price and service quality combinations as it was with 1992 services and rates.[13]

12. J. R. Hicks, "Consumers' Surplus and Index Numbers," *Review of Economic Studies,* vol. 9 (1941–42), pp. 126–37.
13. Because our model was estimated from 1992 survey responses, our estimates of compensating variation are focused on 1992 as the basis of welfare comparison. Consequently, we could not measure how much a household in 1983, for instance, would be willing to pay for the opportunity to purchase cable services at 1992 prices and quality levels. Even if we observed 1983 data, it would be difficult to measure compensating variation for increases in the quality of cable services that were beyond anything available

Changes in cable characteristics may lead to welfare changes that differ from household to household. In the sections that follow, we employ two measures of welfare change associated with changes in cable characteristics. The first is the expected compensating variation associated with changing cable characteristics. This is the expected value of the payment to each household, including both those that subscribe to cable and those that do not, to make each household as well off with the altered cable characteristics—numbers of channels and cable rates—as under the 1992 conditions. The second is the expected value of the additional change in basic cable rates that would result in consumers being just as well off (a compensating variation equal to zero) with these changes in cable service characteristics.

Compensating Variation for Changes in Service Characteristics

With our estimated multinomial logit model of demand for cable service, we measured household compensating variation associated with changes in cable system characteristics. The first row of table 3-2 shows the distribution for our sample of households of compensating variation associated with a $1.00 increase in the monthly basic fee.[14] The expected compensating variation associated with a $1.00 increase in basic cable fees is $.68 in 1992 dollars. The compensating variation varies by household between $.23 and $.93 depending on demographic, cable system, and geographic characteristics.[15] It would require $.68 a month for households in our sample to be compensated for their loss in consumer surplus caused by a $1.00 increase in cable rates. The compensating variation required for a $1.00 decrease in cable rates is almost symmetrically reversed. Our results are confirmed by a calculation of compensating variation for 1990 cable subscribers relative to 1984 cable subscribers based on a model and parameter estimates developed by Robert. N. Rubinovitz.[16] Based on the

---

at any price in 1983.

14. Technically, these values are the expenditure function associated with the estimated multinomial logit model and the actual values of the model evaluated at each household in the sample. The estimates do not include any of the variance of the fitted values associated with the variance-covariance matrix of the parameter estimates. See appendix B for details.

15. The compensating variation from a $1.00 price increase is less than $1.00 because many households do not subscribe to cable, and even those that do subscribe have the option of canceling their subscription.

16. Robert N. Rubinovitz, "Market Power and Price Increases for Basic Cable Service Since Deregulation," *RAND Journal of Economics,* vol. 24 (Spring 1993), pp. 1–18. See appendix A for the derivation of welfare change.

Table 3-2. *Monthly Compensating Variation for Households as the Result of Changes in Cable Service Characteristics*
1992 dollars

Change in cable characteristic	Authors' model				Rubinovitz's estimate at the sample mean
	Mean	Standard deviation	Minimum value	Maximum value	
Increase of $1.00 in basic fee	0.68	0.14	0.23	0.93	0.58
Decrease of $1.00 in basic fee	(0.69)	0.13	(0.93)	(0.24)	(0.63)
Increase of $1.00 in premium fee	0.28	0.13	0.03	0.70	n.a.
Decrease of $1.00 in premium fee	(0.29)	0.13	(0.71)	(0.04)	n.a.
Increased carriage of one basic satellite channel	(0.71)	0.14	(0.96)	(0.24)	(0.63)
Decreased carriage of one basic satellite channel	0.70	0.14	0.24	0.96	0.68
Increased carriage of one basic broadcast channel	(0.94)	0.19	(1.31)	(0.34)	(0.16)
Decreased carriage of one basic broadcast channel	0.92	0.19	0.32	1.31	0.18
Increase of one competing broadcast channel	1.12	0.28	0.41	1.84	n.a.
Decrease of one competing broadcast channel	(1.16)	0.28	(1.87)	(0.44)	n.a.

Source: Authors' calculations.
n.a. Not available.

parameters of his model, we estimate a compensating variation of $.58 from a $1.00 increase in basic fees, well within the range of the estimates from our model.

Using the same methodology, we find that the estimated compensating variation for a $1.00 increase in premium rates is only $.28, far smaller than the compensating variation for an increase in basic fees. This reflects the likelihood that fewer households subscribe to premium service.

Our results demonstrate that cable operators in 1992 had not yet saturated consumer demand for either basic satellite networks or off-air signals. The fifth row of table 3-2 displays the distribution of compensating variation that results from the addition of one basic satellite network in 1992. The average variation from this additional channel is − $.71, and the estimated values range between − $.24 and − $.96. That is, households would be equally well off with the 1992 cable offerings or with the same offering plus an additional basic satellite network and an additional payment of $.71.[17]

The average estimated compensating variation from the carriage of an additional off-air broadcast channel from any geographic market, holding other factors constant, is − $.94 cents. In other words, the average value to households of an additional broadcast station is somewhat higher than that of another basic satellite network, a result consistent with observed audience shares. In contrast, the Rubinovitz model yields a compensating variation of only − $.16 cents for an additional broadcast station. The difference may reflect the inclusion in our model of the broadcast signals that a household can receive without cable.[18] The expected compensating variation from an additional competing local off-air broadcast signal is $1.12, reflecting the fact that another off-air broadcast signal available to consumers without cable reduces the attractiveness of cable options and yields a positive compensating variation. Our model also provides the common-sense result that adding a broadcast signal to a given geographical market and including it in the local cable system's menu reduces the value of cable to the average household, that is, it yields a positive compensating variation of $1.12 − $.94 = $.18.

Changes in Basic Service Fees to Equilibrate Willingness to Pay

Table 3-3 presents changes in basic fees that, in combination with changes in the quality of cable service, would just equilibrate compensating variation to zero. The first row shows that households would be indifferent between the 1992 cable options and an increase in basic fees of $1.03 in combination with one additional basic satellite network. The Rubinovitz model yields a similar value.

This measure of consumer willingness to pay for an additional satellite network is substantially greater than the Federal Communications Com-

17. Estimates from Rubinovitz's model in "Market Power and Price Increases" are very similar.
18. These are defined as all signals available to a household at a grade B contour level or better.

Table 3-3. *Expected Monthly Changes in Basic Cable Subscription Rates to Equilibrate Compensating Variation for Households to Zero as the Result of Changes in Cable Service Characteristics*
1992 dollars

Change in cable characteristics	Author's model mean	Rubinovitz model estimate at the sample mean
Increased carriage of one basic satellite channel	$1.03	$1.10
Decreased carriage of one basic satellite channel	($1.03)	($1.08)
Increased carriage of one basic broadcast channel (no change in competing signals)	$1.35	$0.26
Decreased carriage of one basic broadcast channel (no change in competing signals)	($1.35)	($0.28)
Increased carriage of one basic broadcast channel (increase of one competing signal)	($0.31)	n.a.
Decreased carriage of one basic broadcast channel (decrease of one competing signal)	$0.31	n.a.

Source: Authors' calculations.
n.a. Not available.

mission allows cable operators to charge either under its 1994 benchmark formula or its 1995 going-forward rules. The going-forward rules allow cable operators to recover at most $.20 per month per subscriber for each additional channel plus the license fee.[19] The total amount is likely to be less than the lowest value placed on satellite channels by any household in the sample. The FCC's rules perversely undermine consumer welfare: incentives for cable operators to expand satellite networks are much weaker than the valuation placed on those channels by most households. Under these circumstances, cable operators are unlikely to reach a social optimum at which incremental or marginal costs just equal marginal utility to consumers.

The discrepancy between the FCC's going-forward rules and consumer welfare is even greater for broadcast signals. The third row of table 3-3 shows the willingness of households in our 1992 sample to pay for one additional basic off-air broadcast signal with no change in the number of competing local signals. Households are expected to be indifferent to an increase in basic fees of $1.35 and carriage of one additional preexisting broadcast channel. However, if a new local broadcast station is carried by

19. The total amount is to be capped at $1.50 for six additional channels a year; see 10 FCC Rcd 1226 (1995).

cable, the increased broadcast competition results on balance in households' being less willing to pay for the expanded cable offerings.

The Change in Economic Welfare since 1983–84

Between 1983, the year before cable deregulation was passed, and 1992, cable rates and the quality of cable programming services increased markedly.[20] Did the increase in quality compensate consumers for the higher prices they were charged? The multinomial logit demand model can help answer this question both by a measurement of the change in the probability of subscribing to cable service and through a more formal measure of change in consumer welfare.

For the 279 households in our sample that were served in 1992 by a cable system that was in operation in 1983–84, we compared the likelihood that they would subscribe to the 1992 system (based on cable rates and services) with the likelihood that they would subscribe to the 1983–84 system.[21] For both periods we arbitrarily used 1992 local characteristics, such as the number of broadcast signals available. The results of the comparison are shown in table 3-4. Clearly, the 1992 system characteristics induce a substantial increase in the probability of subscribing either to basic-only service or to basic-plus-premium service. This result is consistent with the empirical finding that cable penetration rates were much higher in 1992 than in 1983–84 despite increases in cable rates.

For the 279 households in our 1992 sample that were passed by cable systems that were in service in 1983–84, we calculated the compensating variation for households offered the rate-service combinations available in 1983–84 rather than those available in 1992. We estimate that the average household would have suffered an average monthly loss in welfare of

---

20. In the congressional hearings preceding passage of the 1992 act, the principal complaints about cable operators concerned their rate increases and their inattention to customer problems with signal quality and outages, new service applications, or confusion and misunderstandings over rates. We have not been able to measure these effects on quality of service.

21. See appendix B for a discussion of the 1983–84 and 1992 cable system characteristics facing each household in our sample. The data for the period before deregulation are drawn from Warren Publishing, *Television and Cable Factbook,* and are for a period spanning 1983–84 because it was impossible to obtain the relevant data solely for 1983.

Table 3-4. *Sensitivity of the Sample Mean of the Likelihood of Household Cable Subscription to 1983–84 and 1992 Cable System Characteristics*

Percent

Choice	Sample mean based on 1983–84 system and 1992 household characteristics	Sample mean based on 1992 system and 1992 household characteristics	Percentage change in the sample means (column 2– column 1/column 1	Expected change in the likelihood of cable choice across all households
No service	38.1	30.0	−21.3	−20.7
Basic service only	36.9	39.9	8.1	10.2
Basic plus premium service	25.0	30.1	20.4	27.4

Source: Authors' calculations based on a sample of 279 households in 1992 served by cable systems that were in operation in 1983–84.

$5.47 in 1992 if faced with the 1983–84 conditions.[22] This value translates into an average loss of $65.00 annually per household for all households, both those that subscribe and those that do not. This result suggests that the approximately 100 million U.S. households in 1992 would have been willing to pay $6.5 billion to obtain the 1992 service-rate combination rather than the 1983–84 combination. In other words, even after paying the higher rates, households were collectively $6.5 billion a year better off with cable's services in 1992 than with those of 1983–84.

There is considerable variation about this mean. Table 3-5 shows changes in monthly welfare by household percentile rank. Slightly more

Table 3-5. *Monthly Changes in 1992 Welfare If Households Were Faced with 1983–84 Cable Service*

1992 dollars

Percentile of households	Change in welfare	Percentile of households	Change in welfare
5th	−13.94	75th	−2.58
10th	−11.54	90th	0.17
25th	−7.86	95th	1.52
50th	−4.78		

Source: Authors' calculations based on a sample of 279 households in 1992 served by cable systems that were in operation in 1983–84.

22. See appendix B for the derivation of welfare change. This welfare analysis, based on an analysis of household data, is buttressed by a similar finding from the demand study by Rubinovitz, "Market Power and Price Increases," that may be used to estimate that

than 10 percent of households would actually have been better off under 1983–84 service characteristics than with 1992 service characteristics. Meanwhile, more than 10 percent of households would have had monthly welfare losses in excess of $10.00.[23]

Price Sensitivity of Demand

Although the model shows that households place considerable value on small changes in cable prices and service quality as measured by compensating variation, demand for service is widely believed to be relatively insensitive to changes in prices. One explanation is that many households value cable services at either far more or far less than the actual rates charged by cable operators. Because subscription to basic cable is a yes-or-no decision, changes in prices and system characteristics may not directly affect subscription decisions in many households but will lead to direct changes in consumer welfare as measured through willingness to pay for the service.

The assumption that consumer demand responds to changes in prices is fundamental to the rate regulation of cable television. What does our model reveal about the sensitivity of cable demand to price? We begin to answer this question by examining the effect of basic cable rates on the demand for cable services.[24] The first column of table 3-6 shows the expected distribution of subscription choices. Based on actual household and cable system characteristics, the model shows the average likelihood of no cable subscription is 31.7 percent, the likelihood of a basic-only subscription is 39.5 percent, and the likelihood of a basic-plus-premium subscription is 28.8 percent. There is considerable variation around these sample averages that reflects differences in household, geographic, and system characteristics.[25]

---

monthly household welfare improved by $5.99 (in 1992 dollars) between 1984 and 1990.

23. See appendix B for the derivation of the welfare change.

24. We examine the sensitivity of cable demand to other factors in appendix B.

25. The calculated probability of no cable subscription for a household has a sample standard deviation of 13.6 percent and ranges from a minimum of 6.7 percent to a maximum of 76.6 percent. The probability of basic-only subscription has a standard deviation of 14.7 percent and ranges from 7.7 percent to 81.9 percent. Similarly, the estimated probability of subscribing to both basic and premium cable has a standard deviation of 13.1 percent with a minimum of 3.6 percent and a maximum of 70.3 percent.

Table 3-6. *Sensitivity of the Sample Mean of the Likelihood of Cable Subscription to Changes in Basic Cable Fees, Holding Other Factors Constant*
Percent

Choice	Sample mean based on actual system and household characteristics	Sample mean based on actual system and household characteristics with 10 percent basic fee increase	Sample mean based on actual system and household characteristics with 10 percent basic fee decrease	Sample mean based on actual system and household characteristics with 17 percent basic fee decrease
No service	31.7	34.1	29.5	28.0
Basic service only	39.5	38.9	39.9	40.2
Basic plus premium service	28.8	27.1	30.5	31.8

Source: Authors' calculations based on a survey of 441 households.

All cable subscribers pay basic fees, and consequently an increase in basic rates would be expected to reduce the number of both basic-only and basic-plus-premium subscribers. If basic cable fees were to increase by 10 percent, holding other factors constant, the average likelihood of not subscribing would increase to 34.1 percent, or by roughly 7.5 percent. The decrease would come partly from basic-only subscribers and more heavily from basic-plus-premium subscribers. Conversely, a 10 percent reduction in cable rates, holding other factors constant, would reduce likelihood of noncable households to 29.5 percent, again approximately a 7.5 percent decrease. The share of cable subscribers increases (or decreases) by approximately 8 percent in response to a 10 percent decrease (or increase) in cable rates. These results indicate an elasticity of demand for cable services to the price of a basic cable package of − 0.8 at our sample mean.[26] The sensitivity of demand to changes in basic cable fees can be very different depending on household and local characteristics.

Between 1986 and 1992, when rates were unregulated, real rates for basic service increased by an average of 50 percent. If all other relevant demand factors had remained constant, our model would have predicted

26. This is not an exact elasticity measure because it is not measuring the demand response to a price change in a single market. Rather, it is the change in the average likelihood of household demand measured across many households in different markets while holding other measurable demand factors constant. The elasticity of demand in a specific cable system would depend on the characteristics of that system and the distribution of demographic characteristics within its service community.

a substantial decrease in the number of subscribers. Yet subscriptions increased (see chapter 2). The only reasonable explanation is that other factors influencing demand, such as the number and quality of satellite-delivered channels, did not remain constant, and they changed in such a way as to increase demand despite the rate increases.

An estimated price elasticity of demand for basic cable service of less than unity implies that many cable operators, if they had market power, could have increased prices profitably in 1992. That they failed to do so has several possible explanations. First, our model may be misspecified— for example, by failing to account for the prices of theater, sports events, and all other relevant substitutes—such that we have systematically under-estimated the own-price elasticity of demand. Alternatively, cable operators may have feared that new price-disciplining sources of competition or regulation were on the horizon. Or because they have many delicately balanced sources of revenue, raising basic rates may have compromised other potential revenue from premium services, equipment rentals, pay-per-view, and advertising.

The FCC's initial round of rate regulation in 1993 called for approximately a 10 percent reduction in regulated revenue.[27] If this round had resulted in a 10 percent decrease in the rates for regulated cable services, and if other factors, including the quality of cable services, had remained constant, we would have expected to see an overall increase in cable subscriptions of 8 percent. An FCC survey found that between April and September 1993 rates for basic programming services fell about 1.5 percent and basic service packages carried 1.8 more channels.[28] Although the commission did not report the change in average national market penetration between 1992 and 1993, the number of subscribers is estimated to have increased by 3.6 percent, very close to our model prediction of 3 percent under these conditions.[29]

The 1994 FCC rate regulations called for a 17 percent eventual across-the-board reduction of regulated rates. When it is fully implemented, if other influences on demand remain constant, the number of basic cable subscriptions should increase by 5.5 percent, consistent with the last column in table 3-6. But other factors, particularly the quality of service, un-

27. Cable operators tended to meet the 10 percent target by reducing the rental and installation rates on equipment rather than reducing programming fees.

28. Federal Communications Commission, Cable Services Bureau, "FCC Cable Regulation Impact Survey Changes in Cable Television Rates Between April 5, 1993–September 1, 1993: Report and Summary," February 1994, p. 4.

29. Paul Kagan Associates, *Kagan Media Index,* April 24, 1995.

doubtedly will not remain constant because of the offsetting effects of regulation and digital-compression technology. It is too soon to test our model against this exogenous shock to cable rates and service quality.[30]

Has Deregulation Improved Consumer Welfare?

Our analysis indicates that most households were better off with the cable television choices available in 1992 than with those available in 1986, not surprising in a market with rapidly changing technology. How much of this improvement in welfare is attributable to deregulation of cable prices and how much to other factors?

The deregulation of cable prices under the 1984 Cable Act did not result in two groups of cable systems, one regulated and the other unregulated, which would have been a natural experimental basis to examine the effects of deregulation. Under the FCC's guidelines requiring three local broadcast signals for a cable system to be considered as facing effective competition, practically all systems were freed from rate regulation. For those few that could still have faced regulation after 1986, no evidence indicates that local authorities actively pursued rate regulation. No information has been compiled on the local regulation permitted after the change in the FCC's definition of effective competition in 1991. Consequently, for practically all cable systems, the effects of deregulation on cable prices and the quality of service from the mid-1980s through 1992 are confounded with changes in technology, an unmeasurable proportion of which would have developed even without deregulation.

The potential contribution of deregulation to consumer welfare depends on the extent to which prices were influenced by regulation in the early and mid-1980s. As we described in chapter 2, price regulation of cable television varied substantially from community to community before the Cable Act of 1984. Consequently, we would expect that the effect of deregulation on welfare would also vary by community.

Allocating some portion of the change in consumer welfare to deregulation is not simply a mechanical exercise of attributing more to deregulation in each community that actually experienced rate regulation. The mere presence of regulation in the 1980s is insufficient to determine whether

30. See chapter 4 for a discussion of recent changes in rates and numbers of subscribers. The evidence through early 1995 does not suggest that the rate reductions have increased enrollments.

rates were indeed influenced by it. The threat of regulation may have disciplined rates in communities without formal regulation. Or regulation may not have constrained prices below levels they would have reached otherwise. Considering data from an FCC survey of cable system characteristics in 1986 and holding all other factors constant, we find no significant differences between franchises subject to regulation and those not subject in the total number of cable channels, basic satellite channels, local broadcast stations carried, basic channels offered, or the price charged for basic service (see appendix A).

Premium services have never been subject to systematic rate regulation. Thus it is not surprising that before 1986 regulation of basic cable services did not have any apparent effect on premium rates. The systems subject to regulation in the FCC sample did not have systematically higher or lower rates than did their unregulated counterparts. Thus regulation before 1986 was not imposed to benefit consumers of basic cable services at the expense of those desiring a richer mix of premium and basic services. Regulation seems not to have reflected a populist strategy of restraining the rates for households able to afford only basic services while allowing premium rates to be sufficiently high to recover some of the costs of basic service.[31]

Still, some evidence suggests that there were behavioral differences between formerly regulated and unregulated cable systems after deregulation. Where deregulation unleashed a previously constrained cable operator, we would expect to observe greater changes in cable rates and cable channel lineups than where deregulation did not remove impediments to operators' decisions. After testing this idea, we found that after deregulation, and holding other factors constant, formerly regulated franchises tended to increase the number of basic satellite channels they offered, and they raised basic fees more than did unregulated franchises.[32]

One cannot, however, infer from these results a precise allocation of the contribution of deregulation to the change in consumer welfare. The extent to which deregulation affected investment and other allocative decisions by cable program producers, networks, equipment suppliers, advertisers, and operators remains unmeasured and unmeasurable. Changes in con-

---

31. This theory was suggested to us by Paul MacAvoy.

32. The data are from "FCC Cable TV Rate Survey Database: Structure of Database and Explanatory Notes," MM Docket no. 92-266, March 30, 1994. The FCC collected information as of November 1986, the eve of deregulation. It is possible, however, that by late 1986 many local regulatory authorities had effectively released cable companies from regulation without formally deregulating them. Thus many regulated systems in the FCC sample may already have been deregulated.

sumer welfare resulting from these decisions may have been as great as from the direct measurable changes in prices and quality of program service.[33]

Even if it were possible to attribute a specific portion of the change in consumer welfare between 1986 and 1992 to deregulation, it would not be possible to make reasonable inferences about specific changes in consumer welfare as a result of reregulation under the Cable Act of 1992. The centralized, uniform regulation under the act bears little resemblance to the localized regulation that prevailed before the Cable Act of 1984.

Deregulation and Capital Investment in Cable Television

The effect of regulation on capital investment in the cable industry has not been studied very much. Unfortunately, the only extensive time-series data on industry investment flows and capital stocks are those published by the Department of Commerce for radio and television. Given the maturity of the radio and television broadcasting industry, it is reasonable to assume that much of the increase in investment reflects the growth of cable, not broadcasting. Figure 3-1 shows a sharp upturn in real investment flows after 1978. This coincides almost exactly with the FCC's decision to revoke its cable signal carriage rules and follows by about two years the Supreme Court's surprise decision revoking the commission's rules for premium programming (see chapter 1). However, rate deregulation did not appear to generate another surge after the 1984 Cable Act or after 1986, when deregulation became effective.[34] Thus the draconian FCC controls on service quality that were in place before the late 1970s would seem to have been far more effective in restraining investment than was the generally loose municipal and state regulation before 1986.

The Exercise of Market Power

Our findings of increased consumer welfare do not indicate whether cable operators could have exercised market power or did exercise it in the 1980s

33. Improvements in the quality of programming on an individual channel, such as ESPN, result from allocative decisions that were not captured in our measure of quality, which was a simple count of the number of satellite networks and off-air channels.

34. A time-series regression analysis of the trend in investment from 1960 through 1993 shows that the real capital stock (lagged one year) and a time dummy that begins with 1979 have highly significant positive coefficients, but that time trends for 1960–78 and 1984–92 or 1986–92 are statistically insignificant.

Figure 3-1. *Gross Investment in Radio, Broadcast Television, and Cable Television, 1970–94*

Billions of 1987 dollars

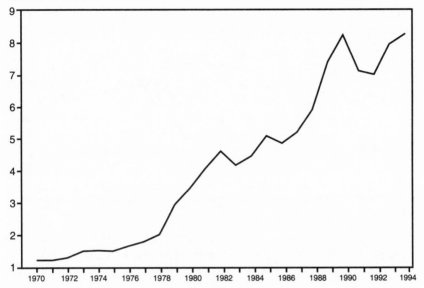

Source: Bureau of Economic Analysis, "Fixed Nonresidential Private Capital by Industry" (May 1995).

and early 1990s. Consumer welfare could have improved under a variety of market structures. The exercise of market power is often considered a necessary condition for rate regulation, but it is far from sufficient, particularly when consumer welfare has improved markedly without regulation.

To measure market power unambiguously, one must identify demand precisely and distinguish it from supply conditions. Our model of household demand avoids the identification problems commonly encountered by other studies of demand for cable services.[35] We do not observe, however, the cost structure of cable firms or others providing competing services. From our demand model, we can trace the price-choice trade-offs made by households in selecting services, but we cannot directly measure whether the market equilibrium is the outcome of pure competition, pure monopoly, or market structures between these two extremes.[36] For many

35. Other models of cable demand are reviewed in appendix A.
36. Economically meaningful cost data by cable system are not publicly available. Economic studies that claim to measure directly the exercise of market power by cable operators have relied on crude and hopelessly inaccurate proxies of cost. See, for example, Rubinovitz, "Market Power and Price Increases," pp. 1–18.

industries the absence of meaningful cost data is not unusual, and the most common means of examining market power are q ratios, price comparisons between firms presumably subject to competition and those that are not, or bounding values based on demand elasticities. We examined the first two of these approaches in chapter 2. Now we examine demand elasticities.

The potential to exercise market power is often linked to the elasticity of demand for cable.[37] For a single-product company operating in a given time period, the inverse of the absolute value of the demand elasticity is equal to the Lerner index: a price-cost ratio consisting of price minus marginal cost divided by price. Lerner indexes are difficult to measure directly because the information necessary to measure marginal cost—and even average cost curves for contestable markets—for a firm is often unobservable.[38] Instead, the Lerner index is often measured implicitly as the inverse ratio of the measured demand elasticity under an assumption of monopoly pricing.

A single-product company facing inelastic demand could exercise additional market power by profitably raising prices.[39] A single-product company facing elastic demand may not be able to raise prices profitably, although it may already have raised prices above competitive levels. The empirical literature on elasticities of demand for basic cable service provides support for the existence of both inelastic and elastic demand. The FCC has reviewed some of these results and has found own-price elasticities of demand for basic cable with absolute values ranging from 0.8 to 3.75.[40] Our findings are even below the lower end of that range.[41]

37. 9 FCC Rcd 7442 (1994).

38. Under current FCC regulations, most cable franchises are required to report considerable amounts of cost information. Even this information, however, is often insufficient to measure true economic marginal and average costs. Only costs for regulated services, not potentially joint but unregulated services, are reported. It is also difficult to allocate multisystem operator costs to individual systems. Another difficulty is that cable operators use different accounting conventions. Even if these problems could be surmounted, each system may have unique circumstances and a slightly different but rapidly changing technology. A true instantaneous marginal cost for each system would probably not be identifiable.

39. As we discuss later, in setting prices for a service a multiproduct company must take into account consumer demand for the substitute and complementary services it offers.

40. 9 FCC Rcd 7442 (1994), p. H-11.

41. This result of inelastic household demand for basic cable services contrasts sharply with earlier findings by Robert Crandall: own-price elasticity of demand for basic services with an absolute value as high as 3.4. See "Elasticity of Demand for Cable Services and the Effect of Broadcast Signals on Cable Prices," paper appended to *TCI Reply Comments* in MM Docket no. 90-4, April 6, 1990. See appendix A for an explanation of why measures of demand elasticities may differ.

Our findings indicate that any opportunity operators may have had to exercise market power over basic cable rates was not fully exploited in either 1992 or 1993. This result would be truly puzzling if operators offered only basic service. But basic service in 1992 and today provides access to premium and other services. The relationships between price and demand conditions for multiproduct firms with market power is less clear than for firms with a single product. A firm might price some products along an inelastic portion of the demand curve so as to increase sales of complementary products. By so doing, for example, a cable company might sell additional subscriptions to a basic service at a loss to attract additional subscribers to premium and pay-per-view services and equipment rentals.

Other forces may also have disciplined rates for basic cable to remain along the inelastic portion of demand curves. Dynamic considerations may also lead a firm to price along an inelastic portion of a demand curve today to develop customer loyalty so as to preserve or increase future sales. Even the fear of future regulation or new competitors may have disciplined prices.[42]

Our demand model indicates that cable operators in 1992 could have profitably raised prices for basic cable services. The choice not to exercise potential market power fully may have resulted from many factors, but all of them undermine any urgent necessity for rate regulation. Reregulation of basic cable services in 1992 could not be justified as a rolling back of rates that reflected the full exercise of market power over access to basic services. Even without regulation, the opportunity of cable operators to exploit any market power has been and will continue to be eroded by direct broadcast satellites and other new technologies.

Conclusion

Supporters of the Cable Act of 1992 were wont to compare 1992 unregulated cable prices and services unfavorably with those that prevailed before the Cable Act of 1984, and they concluded that a return to regulation was in consumers' interest. Indeed, the language of the act contains just such an unfavorable comparison.[43] This comparison, however, failed to consider that better service could have more than offset any increase in rates attributable to deregulation. Although available information does not per-

---

42. Our results already account for the effects of competition from broadcast signals.
43. *The Cable Television Consumer Protection and Competition Act of 1992*, sec. 2.

mit a precise statement of how much better or worse off consumers would have been under regulation rather than deregulation, we find that most consumers were much better off with the available cable offerings in 1992 than with those of 1984.

In implementing price regulation under the 1992 act, the FCC failed to recognize the value households place on the quality of cable service. A subscriber would be far better off paying a dollar a month for an additional basic channel than not being offered the channel at all. Rather than encouraging the expansion of basic service, the FCC has set rates for additional channels that are far below their value to most consumers. The possibility that regulation will inhibit the development of new services in this rapidly changing industry, however, has been reduced by the 1996 Telecommunications Act that once again deregulates most cable rates by 1999.

CHAPTER FOUR

The Cable Industry under Regulation

T HE Cable Television Consumer Protection and Competition Act was passed over President Bush's veto in late 1992. Regulations began appearing in 1993, but their effects were probably felt much earlier. Indeed, the impact on cable television companies may have been anticipated well before January 1992 when the Senate passed the bill that was to form the basis for the final legislation. In this chapter, we examine the influence of the proposed and actual new regulatory regimes on cable company shares, acquisition prices, and service rates.

The opening blow in the cable reregulation effort was landed by the General Accounting Office in August 1989 when it released its first report on cable rate increases. The report created so much political controversy that the chairman of the Telecommunications Subcommittee of the House Energy and Commerce Committee asked on October 2 for a second study, which was released in June 1990. This report confirmed that both cable rates and the number of channels had increased since deregulation.[1]

The Senate and House Commerce Committees reported out bills authorizing reregulation of basic cable rates in June 1990.[2] The House bill passed on a voice vote in September, but the Senate bill (S. 1880) failed to come to the floor. When a new Congress convened in 1991, cable legislation was reintroduced. The legislation was not in doubt in the House, but it had to clear several hurdles in the Senate. In May 1991 a bill was reported out of the Senate Commerce Committee by a margin of 16–3. By late 1991, passage seemed certain, and on January 31, 1992, the Senate voted for it 73–18. The House followed in June.[3]

1. General Accounting Office, *National Survey of Cable Television Rates and Services,* GAO/R CED 89-193 (August 1989); and GAO, *Follow-Up National Survey of Cable Television Rates and Services,* GAO/RCED 90-199 (June 1990).

2. Alison Pytte,"Cable TV Reregulation Bill Sweeps by Senate Panel," *Congressional Quarterly,* vol. 48 (June 9, 1990), pp. 1786–87; and Pytte, "Cable Reregulation Measure Moves Forward in House," *Congressional Quarterly,* vol. 48 (June 30, 1990), p. 2053.

3. See Congressional Quarterly, *CQ Almanac,* vol. 47 (1991), p. 158; and vol. 48 (1992), p. 171.

Table 4-1. *Average Monthly Rates of Return from Cable MSO Common Equities and All Stocks, 1984–94*
Percent

	Period			
Company	Jan. 1984– June 1989	July 1989– June 1990	July 1990– Dec. 1991	Jan. 1992– Dec. 1994
TCI	0.030	−0.014	0.017	0.011
Comcast	0.024	−0.008	0.018	0.017
Cablevision Systems	0.033	−0.034	0.035	0.018
Viacom	0.046	0.009	0.022	0.011
TCA	0.026	−0.019	0.015	0.011
Century Communications	0.047	−0.033	0.048	−0.0003
Falcon Cable	0.012	−0.027	−0.002	−0.0006
Adelphia Communications	0.025	−0.057	0.062	−0.009
All stocks	0.014	0.014	0.013	−0.005

Source: Authors' calculations based on data from The Monthly Stock File at the Center for Research on Security Prices, Graduate School of Business, University of Chicago, 1993; and Ibbotson Associates, *Stocks, Bonds, Bills, Inflation Yearbook* (Chicago, 1994).

Cable Company Common Equities

Given the lopsided Senate committee vote in May 1991, one might have expected investors to begin reacting even before then to the likelihood of reregulation. Alternatively, final passage by a margin sufficient to override a possible presidential veto may not have been apparent to investors until shortly before the January 1992 vote. We examined both possibilities by analyzing the returns from holding the common equities of eight listed stocks of multiple service operators for various periods beginning in July 1989, one month before the release of the first GAO report.[4]

We begin with a comparison of the average monthly rates of return for holders of major MSO equities for various periods between January 1984 and June 1993 (table 4-1). From January 1984 to June 1989 the average monthly return to the owners of the equities in the eight companies was generally much higher than the 1.4 percent average monthly return on all stocks in the period. TCI, Cablevision Systems, Viacom, and Century Communications realized returns more than double the market average.[5] In the next twelve months, however, every MSO except Viacom experi-

4. We analyze the returns for companies that are primarily cable television firms. We did not include heavily diversified companies such as Time Warner and Times Mirror. It should be noted, however, that even those equities listed in table 4-1 do not represent firms that are purely cable operators.
5. Some of the averages shown in table 4-1 are for periods shorter than five and one-half years because their equities were not listed over the entire time.

Table 4-2. *Riskiness of Cable MSO Common Equities, 1984–94*

Company	Period			
	Jan. 1984– *June 1989*	*July 1989–* *June 1990*	*July 1990–* *Dec. 1991*	*Jan. 1992–* *Dec. 1994*
TCI	1.31	1.60	1.89	1.65
Comcast	1.11	1.86	1.00	2.31
Cablevision Systems	1.26	1.12	2.79	1.77
Viacom	1.84	1.81	1.64	0.79ª
TCA	0.90	0.86	1.12	2.11
Century Communications	1.58	2.07	2.66	2.68
Falcon Cable	0.32	0.10ª	0.75ª	1.05ª
Adelphia Communications	1.29	2.19	2.44	3.32
All stocks	1.0	1.0	1.0	1.0

Source: See table 4-1. Estimated β from capital-asset pricing model.
ªNot statistically different from zero at the 5 percent confidence level.

enced negative returns, even though the stock market continued to enjoy average returns of 1.4 percent a month. The difference in performance between the cable equities and the overall market was enormous in some cases, as much as 7 percent a month, or in excess of 125 percent a year. The market was apparently reacting to the political attention being focused in 1989–90 on cable rate increases, attention that would culminate in reregulation bills being reported out of the House and Senate committees in June 1990.

After June 1990, cable equities generally experienced returns exceeding those in the overall market, but beginning from a base that had been severely depressed during the previous twelve months. Indeed, in 1992–93 all the cable equities strongly outperformed the market, even though the Cable Act was passed in late 1992 and the FCC began to regulate in 1993. The stock market in 1989–90 had apparently anticipated and perhaps even overanticipated the effect of regulation.

The effect on the equity market of possible congressional action and subsequent FCC regulation was not limited to a year of negative returns during a bull market. The threat of legislation also affected the relative riskiness of holding these equities. No one could be sure what the final legislation would be or how it would affect industry profitability. As a result, the systematic risk of holding these securities, as measured by the covariance of their returns with the market, β, rose sharply after June 1989.[6] Table 4-2 provides, for each of the eight MSOs during the four periods

6. The risk measure, $β_i$, is the slope coefficient of a regression of the returns on the ith security on the returns from the overall market.

Table 4-3. *Cumulative Excess Returns from Holding Cable MSO Common Equities, July 1989–June 1990*[a]
Percent

System	Excess returns	System	Excess returns
TCI	−0.415	Century	−0.666
Comcast	−0.342	Communications	
Cablevision	−0.580	Falcon	−0.399
Systems		Cable	
Viacom	−0.494	Adelphia	−0.695
TCA	−0.451	Communications	

Source: Authors' calculations from CAP model estimated over January 1984 to June 1989.
a. Estimates reflect the difference between actual (r_{it}) and predicted returns (p_{it}) from the CAP model cumulated over the July 1989 to June 1990 period, or $[\Pi(1 + r_{it} - p_{it})] - 1$.

shown in table 4-1, the estimates of β from the standard capital-asset pricing (CAP) model.[7] Four of the eight experienced an increase in β after June 1989, and the β estimates for every firm except Viacom were higher in 1992–94 than in 1984–89. Thus the market adjusted to the threat of regulation both by reducing the value of cable equities and increasing its discount for the risk of holding them.

One may also use the capital-asset pricing model to provide somewhat more precise estimates of the impact on cable system equities of the events following June 1989. We estimated the CAP model for each equity from January 1984 through June 1989 and used the estimated equation to forecast returns over the ensuing months, given the overall performance of the stock market. The difference between the actual returns and the model's predicted returns were then calculated to determine the impact of exogenous events on the value of each firm's common equity. These residuals, cumulated over the twelve months after June 1989, are shown in table 4-3. The cumulative loss in market value was between 34 and 70 percent as Congress was drafting legislation to reimpose regulation. Weighting these residuals by the relative size of each MSO leads to an average decrease of about 46 percent, a staggering reduction in the value of these companies.[8]

7. Specifically, the form of the capital-asset pricing model used in this analysis is $R_{it} - rfr = \alpha^i + \beta_i(M_t - rfr_t) + u_{it}$, where R_{it} is the rate of return on the ith equity in the *t-th* month, rfr_t is the rate of return on a riskless treasury bill in the *t-th* month, M_t is the return on all stocks in the *t-th* month, and u_i is a random disturbance term. This equation is estimated for monthly returns on each cable equity from the Center for Research in Security Prices tape and average returns on treasury bills and stocks calculated by Ibbotson Associates.

8. Of course, not all of the difference between forecasted and actual prices may be attributable to the threat of reregulation, but we could not identify other forces that would explain the very large drop in the return. No direct broadcast satellites were being launched.

Table 4-4. *Average Nominal and Real Price of Cable System Sales per Existing Subscriber, 1985–94*
Dollars per month unless otherwise specified

Year	Simple average (current dollars)	Simple average[a] (1982–84 dollars)	Weighted average[b] (current dollars)	Weighted average[b] (1982–84 dollars)
1984	924	889	1,015	977
1985	981	912	1,135	1,054
1986	1,228	1,120	1,466	1,338
1987	1,348	1,187	1,541	1,357
1988	1,559	1,318	1,995	1,686
1989	1,884	1,487	2,599	2,096
1990	1,812	1,386	2,130	1,630
1991	1,619	1,189	1,823	1,338
1992	1,637	1,167	1,593	1,135
1993	1,522	1,053	1,716	1,188
1994	1,748	1,178	2,103	1,417

Source: Paul Kagan Associates, *Cable TV Investor* (Carmel, Calif.), random sample.
a. Using the consumer price index for urban workers (CPI-U).
b. Weighted by total basic subscribers.

Thereafter, the average returns on the equities rose once again, but with much higher β's.

Cable Company Acquisition Prices

The profitability of cable operations varies from company to company depending on their portfolios of assets, local market conditions, and management decisions. MSOs also are often heavy investors in programming and other cable-related services. Thus the fate of their equities reflected a variety of forces besides the prospects for cable rate reregulation. However, the prices they paid to acquire operating cable systems may be a good measure of the effects of prospective rate regulation.

The average prices paid for existing cable systems in the period covering deregulation and reregulation are shown in table 4-4 using two measures of the average price per subscriber. The first is a simple average across all sales in the sample of 480 system transactions from 1984 to 1994. The

Telephone companies were not building new broadband networks. There was no slowdown in system growth. Revenues continued to grow at double-digit rates. See Paul Kagan Associates, *Kagan Media Index,* August 3, 1993.

second is a weighted average, reflecting the sum of all purchase prices divided by the sum of all subscribers acquired in each year. These data show the rapid increase in the average sales price per subscriber between 1985 and 1989, when rates were deregulated and the stock market was soaring. The rate of increase was much greater for the weighted average than for the simple average, reflecting the high values paid for a few large systems, and the 1990–93 decline was also much greater.

Whatever the measure, the high prices of cable systems energized the political campaign for reregulation in the 1990s as economists pointed out that the market value of the systems had risen to more than three times the reproduction value of assets.[9] Because much of the value of cable systems probably derives from prospective new services instead of monopoly rents in offering existing services, the 1989 prices paid for a few large systems may have reflected speculative overshooting of the market.[10] After 1990 the real value of acquisition prices began to fall, but they appear to have begun to rise again in 1994.[11] Both measures of real prices fell nearly to 1987 levels, about 13 to 15 percent below the average of their 1988 and 1990 levels, but 21 to 32 percent below their 1989 values. In 1993, prices were 22 to 28 percent below the average of their 1988 and 1990 values, perhaps reflecting investors' apprehension about the FCC's rules implementing the 1992 act.

In chapter 2 we showed that values for cable systems rose by about 20 percent in real terms in 1987 and then by another 20 percent by 1989, after accounting for other forces such as system maturity, market penetration of premium channels, and the real level of stock prices generally. These prices receded to 1984–86 levels after 1990, presumably because of the threat of reregulation, but also perhaps because of the economic downturn of 1990–91 and the emergence of competing delivery technologies (see table 2-1). These results suggest that by 1993 prices had fallen about 29 percent from their peak, a result consistent with table 4-4. Given the subsequent rise in 1994, we conclude that recent events have combined to reduce cable system prices by about 15 to 20 percent.

9. See, for example, Paul W. MacAvoy, "Tobin's q and the Cable Industry's Market Power," in MM Docket no. 89-600, February 28, 1990. app. 5.

10. For a response to MacAvoy, see Robert W. Crandall, "Vertical Integration and q-Ratios in the Cable Industry," paper prepared for TCI, MM Docket no. 89-600, April 2, 1990.

11. Prices are deflated by the CPI-U. The 1994 data are not used in our chapter 2 empirical analysis because the year was incomplete at the time the sample was drawn. Our weighted-average estimate is very close to the FCC's estimate of $2,035 published in 9 FCC Rcd 7442 (1994), p. C-8.

It is impossible know exactly what proportion of these changes in equity values or prices of cable systems can be ascribed to the onset of federal regulation; there are simply too many other factors that may be at work. In the past five years technology has changed dramatically. A direct broadcast satellite service is now offering 150 or more channels. Telephone companies have become exceedingly interested in cable systems outside their own regions as conduits for new services and information. New wireless cable and cellular cable systems are being developed. All these developments surely have an impact on the value of cable systems.[12] But reregulation certainly had some effect. Investors in 1991 and 1992 could not know precisely how reregulation would work in practice. By 1993 the effects were becoming much clearer. The FCC had made important decisions about the level of rates, rules on vertical and horizontal regulation, and the adjustment for inflation. We now turn to the effects of these rules on actual rates.

Subscriber Rates

As described in chapter 2, the FCC implemented cable regulations throughout 1993 and early 1994. Responding to criticisms that it had not reduced rates sufficiently, it published the results of a 1993 survey that remains the most recent comprehensive source of data on the rates subscribers pay (table 4-5). All the most important rates decreased between April, when the initial regulations became effective, and September 1993. The extent of the decrease depended, however, on the type of service offered.

By September 1993, before the FCC mandated the 17 percent rollback, rates for regulated services had declined about 6 percent. The overall rate of reduction in revenue per subscriber, including rates for premium channels and pay-per-view, which are unregulated, was surely much lower. Given that basic and other regulated services account for less than 60 percent of cable revenues, the maximum reduction of revenues from existing customers was probably 10 percent. As we explain in appendix B, these regulated price reductions are likely to have expanded the customer base somewhat, but not by enough to keep revenues constant.

12. We describe these new technologies in chapter 6.

Table 4-5. *Cable Television Rates for Selected Services, April–September 1993*
Dollars per month unless otherwise specified

Level of service	Average rate April 1993	Average rate September 1993	Percent change
Non–cable-ready			
Limited basic plus converter and remote	12.81	12.07	− 5.8
Expanded basic plus converter and remote	25.92	22.93	− 11.5
Expanded basic plus converter and remote, adjusted for à la carte	25.92	24.32	− 6.2
Expanded basic plus converter and remote plus HBO, adjusted for à la carte	37.45	36.22	− 3.3
Cable-ready			
Limited basic plus converter and remote	10.91	11.18	2.5
Expanded basic plus converter and remote	23.75	22.11	− 6.9
Expanded basic plus converter and remote, adjusted for à la carte	23.75	23.62	− 0.5
Expanded basic plus converter and remote plus HBO, adjusted for à la carte	33.60	35.94	− 1.8

Source: Federal Communications Commission Cable Bureau, "FCC Cable Regulation Impact Survey, Changes in Cable Television Rates between April 5, 1993–September 1, 1993," February 1994.

Government estimates of consumer expenditures on cable television suggest a more dramatic effect of regulation (figure 4-1).[13] Real annual spending per subscriber rose steadily from 1982 to 1992 after declining in the previous four years.[14] After 1992, however, spending per subscriber decreased by 6 percent. It is possible to explain 92.3 percent of the variance in the real spending series with a simple time trend. The forecasts from this log-linear trend regression are also shown in figure 4-1. By 1994 the deviation from trend was 8 percent; the decline relative to trend in

13. The expenditure estimates provided by the Bureau of Economic Analysis, April 1994, are divided by A. C. Nielsen estimates of cable subscribers in November of each year as published in National Cable Television Association, *Cable Television Developments,* vol. 19 (Spring 1995), p. 6.

14. The 1978–82 decline probably reflected the surge in inflation at a time when many cable systems were under rate regulation by states or municipalities.

Figure 4-1. *Annual Cable Subscription Revenues per Subscriber, 1975–94*

Constant 1994 dollars

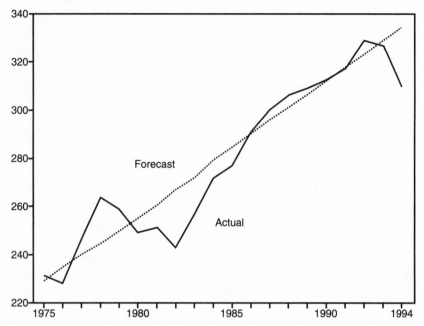

Source: Authors' estimates based on Department of Commerce, Bureau of Economic Analysis, personal consumption expenditure data.

1992–94 was 10 percent.[15] It would appear that exogenous forces, including reregulation, reduced cable system subscriber revenues by nearly 10 percent between 1992 and 1994.

This early evidence suggests that rate reregulation has had a modest effect on cable operator revenues. The impact on cash flows has, however, been much greater. Cash flows have averaged about 45 percent of total revenues.[16] Therefore, a 10 percent reduction in revenues would translate

15. When a dummy variable for 1994 is included with the time trend, the share of the explained variance rises to 96.1 percent and the 1994 dummy variable's coefficient is −0.0784, suggesting that revenues per subscriber fell 7.8 percent relative to the trend in 1994.

16. Paul Kagan Associates, *Cable TV Financial Databook* (Carmel, Calif., June 1993), p. 36, cited in Thomas W. Hazlett, "Regulating Cable Television Rates: An Economic Analysis," working paper prepared for American Enterprise Institute, October 4, 1994.

into a 22 percent reduction in cash flow.[17] This is undoubtedly a worst-case estimate from the standpoint of cable system owners. If regulation is likely to have similar effects on future cash flows, the maximum effect on the present value of cable service companies would also be 22 percent. But cable systems are not being sold simply as vehicles to deliver the current array of one-way consumer video services, and the impact of regulation on new video services will probably be less severe. It is likely, then, that regulation has reduced the value of cable assets by somewhat less than 22 percent.

Earlier we found that the value of cable MSO equities fell by an average of 46 percent in 1989–90. If all of this decline is attributed to the threat of regulation, the anticipated effect of regulation on cable MSO assets would have been to devalue them by about 23 percent, given a debt-equity ratio of 1:1 at market values of equity. The decline in cable equities in 1989–90 therefore appears to have been accurately anticipating the effect of regulation or perhaps the combination of the effects of anticipated regulation, recession, and emerging competition from direct broadcast satellites.

In summary, the value of cable systems decreased by an average of 15 to 20 percent during the period when cable rate regulation was being deliberated and the 1992 Cable Act was being passed. Because we cannot account for all the other possible influences on the value of cable systems, we cannot be sure that even this range is entirely the result of rate reregulation. However, it appears unlikely that the FCC has succeeded in reducing current and future cash flows by 35 percent or more as implied in public announcements of 1993–94 rate rollbacks.[18]

Output and Program Quality

Given that the 1992 Cable Act is only four years old and that cable rates have been regulated for about three years, it is not yet possible to discern

17. Our discussion focuses on the effect of rate regulation on revenues and, ultimately, on after-tax cash flows. Other aspects of regulation mandated by the 1992 Cable Act, such as provisions that systems must carry certain local channels and must set aside channels for leasing by community groups (leased-access requirements), may also have had an effect on cash flows.

18. 9 FCC Rcd 4119 (1994). This is based on the 17 percent rate rollback and the preregulation ratio of cash flows to total revenues.

its effects on program quality or the number of channels offered.[19] Investments in program networks and channel capacity have long lead times; therefore, one would not expect to see much immediate effect on the number of channels offered, the number of program networks, or total programming expenditure.

The National Cable Television Association has reported that the number of cable networks has continued to grow since reregulation.[20] In addition, Paul Kagan Associates estimates that the total expenditures by cable systems on programming continued to increase after 1991, although at a slower rate. Between 1986 and 1991 programming outlays increased at an annual rate of nearly 10 percent; between 1991 and 1994 growth slowed to less than 8 percent annually.[21] This slowdown can be explained as resulting from the 1990–91 recession and its dampening effect on the growth of the number of subscribers. But with competition from direct broadcast satellites appearing in 1994 and the threat of increased competition from telephone companies and wireless cable systems, one might have expected programming outlays to have increased more strongly.[22]

The effects of regulation on cable program development may turn out to be minor. Although lower values of cable system franchises could be expected to reduce the large MSOs' ability to finance new networks, the new regulations may not affect prospective program networks if cable systems are allowed to offer these incremental channels à la carte and unregulated. The FCC is now enmeshed in regulatory decisions regarding future programming expenditures. Initial rules that would have provided little

19. The provisions requiring cable systems to carry all local broadcast signals have likely led to a reallocation of channels for some systems. In addition, some systems may have responded to regulation by shifting some channels from regulated basic service to an unregulated additional package.

20. National Cable Television Association, *Cable Television Developments,* vol. 19 (Spring 1995), p. 6.

21. Paul Kagan Associates, as reported in National Cable Television Association, *Cable Television Developments,* vol. 19 (Spring 1995), p. 7.

22. Thomas Hazlett has contended that the slowing growth of basic cable network viewing since 1990 is a reflection of the reduced programming effort caused by the return of cable rate regulation. Between the 1983–84 and 1990–91 seasons, household viewing of cable networks increased from 17 percent of all viewing to 35 percent, an annual rate of increase of 10 percent. Between 1990–91 and 1993–94, however, the growth rate slowed to less than 2 percent a year. See National Cable Television Association, *Cable Television Developments* (Spring 1995), p. 5. Hazlett interprets this sharp deceleration as a reflection of reduced effort in developing new networks or improving the quality of older ones. Thomas W. Hazlett and Matthew L. Spitzer, *Public Policy toward Cable Television,* vol. 2: *Regulation and the First Amendment* (forthcoming).

incentive for operators to add basic programming channels have been revised to provide at least some incentive for the expansion of programming, although the incentive does not begin to reflect consumer valuation of such programming.[23] And it is not clear that these rules will affect investment in new premium networks or pay-per-view services.

An erosion of competition from nonpremium channels would allow the premium networks to increase their rates again. Paul Kagan Associates has estimated that the average nominal premium cable rate remained between $10.17 and $10.31 a month over the entire 1985–92 period. This means that real charges fell at the rate of inflation, about 3.5 percent over the period.[24] The decline accelerated in 1993–94; rates for premium channels fell to an average of $9.38 a month, nearly 15 percent below their real 1992 prices. This trend may reflect the fact that video cassette rentals are the primary competition for premium channels and the competition is growing more intense.

Surely, the increased volatility and riskiness of cable equities cannot be conducive to investment in new programming or greater channel capacity. But not all the increase in risk can be laid at the feet of the Congress or the FCC. In 1993–94 direct broadcast satellites were launched by Hughes Electronics; Hughes owns one system, DirecTV, and Hubbard owns the other, USSB. Many joint ventures between cable companies and telephone carriers were negotiated, although the largest, the acquisition of TCI by Bell Atlantic, collapsed in part because of cable reregulation.[25] The regional Bell operating companies began a full-scale assault on the law banning telephone company involvement in cable operations that started to bear fruit in 1993 when a federal court overturned it on First Amendment grounds.[26] The rules that cable systems must carry local broadcast signals were pushing some networks off existing cable systems.

At the same time, the likelihood that digital signal compression technologies will lead to an enormous increase in channel capacity within two or three years is stimulating a search for new programming ideas (the cable companies are awaiting the full development of an MPEG2 compression

23. 10 FCC Rcd 1226 (1995). See chapter 3.

24. Paul Kagan Associates, *Marketing New Media* (Carmel, Calif., 1994).

25. There was considerable controversy over the reasons the deal failed. Some claim that the clash in corporate cultures was too much to overcome. Others cite the decrease in projected TCI cash flows caused by the FCC's rules.

26. *Chesapeake and Potomac Telephone Company of Virginia, et. al. v. United States of America*, 830 F. Supp. 909 (E.D. Va. 1993). Appeals are pending on this case, and similar cases are pending in many other federal district courts.

standard that may expand capacity to 500 channels). The Hughes direct broadcast satellite service uses the less ambitious M-PEG1 standard, allowing it to offer perhaps 150 channels. Either format will inevitably encourage greater demand for and supply of programming.

A final source of evidence on the effects of regulation may be found in the FCC's attempt to muster public support for its regulatory program. The commission has argued that by reducing cable rates it is actually encouraging new subscriptions and thus helping the cable industry expand its subscriber base. Unfortunately for the commission, the data on cable subscribers drive one to precisely the opposite conclusion. Growth in the number of subscriptions has slowed markedly even as basic cable rates go down, a reflection of either deteriorating service quality or reduced demand for cable caused by substitute services such as direct broadcast satellites.

As figure 4-2 shows, the number of subscribers grew rapidly from the late 1970s through 1985, undoubtedly due to the newly won freedom of cable operators to expand channel capacity with premium programming and imported broadcast signals as well as to the expansion in basic cable networks made possible by satellite delivery. After 1985 this growth slowed, and the 1990–91 recession contributed to a further slowdown. But growth did not rebound after the economy recovered in 1992–94. In fact, subscribers numbered more than 2 million less than a prediction based on a time trend, a post-1985 trend variable, and real per capita income.[27] No more than 300,000 of the 2 million can be attributed to the direct broadcast satellite service. Given the evidence that basic subscriber rates may have been depressed by as much as 10 percent, the failure even to match the trend should pose a warning to regulators that something may be amiss.

Investment in Cable Companies

The surge of investment in the radio and television sector of the economy during the late 1970s and 1980s (see figure 3-1) implies that the deregula-

---

27. Specifically, the predicted series in figure 4-2 is based on the regression equation: Log (*Subscribers*) = 2.122 + 0.15 *TIME* − 0.11 *TIME* (*Post-1985*) + 0.49 Log (*Real per Capita Income*), where *TIME* and *TIME* (*post-1985*) are time trends for 1975–92 and 1986–92, respectively. Subscriber data are from A. C. Nielsen; the real per capita income series is from the Department of Commerce, Bureau of Economic Analysis, deflated by the CPI. The equation is estimated for 1975–92 and is used to forecast 1993 and 1994. By 1994 the forecast rises to 63.2 million subscribers. Actual subscribers were 60.5 million.

Figure 4-2. *Cable Television Subscribers, 1975–94*

Thousands

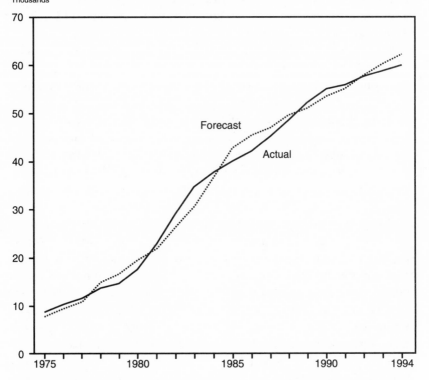

Source: A. C. Neilson Co. in National Cable Television Association, *Cable Television Developments*, vol. 19 (Spring 1995), p. 2; and author's estimates.

tory environment spurred expenditures on new cable systems and expansions of older ones. But this wave stopped in 1990, reflecting a sharp drop in cable equity values. Real investment has failed to climb back to 1990 levels despite the substantial amounts of capital required by some systems to replace older cables with new fiber-optic facilities. Some of the sluggishness might be attributed to the mild 1990–91 recession, but most of it must be considered at least prima facie evidence that the reduction in industry cash flow and the increase in the riskiness of cable equities is taking its toll on investment.

Conclusion

Reregulation has clearly affected cable rates, system cash flows, and therefore the values of systems and MSOs' common equities. Regulation was anticipated by equity markets and resulted in a significant reductions in the value of MSO common equities following the release of the 1989 GAO report that was so critical of the industry. The riskiness of cable equities increased sharply, reflecting the uncertainty over the forthcoming regulatory regime and, undoubtedly, over competition from multichannel video distributors such as direct broadcast satellites and, potentially, telephone companies. Rate regulation appears to have reduced industry revenues by 6 to 10 percent, although the effect on regulated cable rates and revenues could be as much as 17 percent. Cheaper rates have not, however, increased cable subscriptions, leading us to conclude that consumers may have surmised that service quality deteriorated.

It is simply too early to measure the effects of the regulatory program on programming quality. It is also too early to measure the impact of reregulation on viewer choices because cable programming investments have long lead times and are influenced by many other factors in the turbulent video distribution sector. Thus we cannot yet measure the full impacts of regulation on economic welfare. However, our results in chapter 3 suggest that even a small adverse effect on program choices could offset any benefits that consumers received from reduced rates.

CHAPTER FIVE

Effective Competition?

T HE regulatory regime now constraining the cable television industry is a product of decades of unfortunate public policy choices, the natural-monopoly characteristics of a network industry, and the industry's bad public image.[1] Cable was bottled up too long by FCC regulations designed to protect broadcasters and by municipal franchising authorities eager to tap a revenue source. When finally released from both regulatory regimes, the industry rapidly expanded its reach and its services while raising rates and often disregarding customer complaints. As a result, it is widely considered a monopoly that has exploited consumers and is thus a worthy candidate for government regulation. But this monopoly derives in part from government actions explicitly intended to prevent competition, such as those of the FCC, the 1984 Cable Act's ban on telephone company competition with cable, and restrictions by municipal franchising authorities on competition from any source. As the government barriers are now being eliminated, will the multichannel video delivery market become truly competitive and the need for rate regulation evaporate? In this chapter, we evaluate the prospects for contestability in this market.

Competition among Cable Companies

There is no inherent reason why only one cable system should exist in a community. A second system, using the same ducts or telephone poles to carry its distribution plant, could conceivably offer actual and potential competition to many existing cable systems, particularly in areas with substantial population density. Such a strategy clearly involves a duplication of assets that is in a sense unnecessary, but duplication is widespread in other network industries. For example, Federal Express and United Parcel Service duplicate the U.S. Post Office's delivery networks, as do appliance

---

1. Although there may be few network externalities or none, cable systems may be natural monopolies because of the high cost of duplicating distribution facilities.

stores, pizza delivery services, and other businesses.[2] Productive efficiency may be sacrificed in such duplication, but this cost may be more than offset by improvements in consumer welfare that result from potential improvements in the quality of service.

The cost of overbuilding a cable franchise area with a second system is surprisingly modest. Bruce Owen and Peter Greenhalgh estimated that a second system would raise costs per subscriber about 14 percent higher than the levels experienced by an efficient cable monopolist.[3] Service quality would not have to improve much to offset such an increase. Indeed, by simply offering a slightly different mix of basic cable networks, premium networks, pay-per-view services, and broadcast stations from the array now available, a second service might be able to increase viewer welfare by much more than the cost of overbuilding. And by stimulating the incumbent company to be more concerned about ensuring good quality signals and responding to customer complaints, further improvements in economic welfare could be achievable. Finally, overbuilding could reduce rates substantially.

Despite these enticements, fewer than fifty cities have significant competition among cable systems.[4] A 1992 FCC survey to collect data for establishing the regulatory benchmarks under the 1992 Cable Act elicited responses from forty-five overbuilt areas.[5] Given more than 30,000 franchises in the country, overlap is clearly uncommon.[6] But one should not conclude from its absence that it is uneconomical.

Why hasn't more competition emerged? First, cable television systems generally require a franchise from a municipal government. Municipal franchising is often restrictive, favoring the franchisee and some constituency groups. Second, some competitive situations have been ended by mergers or system swaps among MSOs. A 1990 Consumers' Research survey concluded that rates were 18 percent lower in overbuild markets than in those with a single supplier.[7] Our analysis of the FCC's 1992 survey data showed that there were no statistically significant differences in rates

---

2. Admittedly, the share of sunk costs in the total costs of these networks is smaller than it is in the cable industry. Thus duplication of cable networks is less likely than the duplication of these other networks.

3. Bruce M. Owen and Peter R. Greenhalgh, "Competitive Policy Considerations in Cable Television Franchising," *Contemporary Policy Issues,* vol. 4 (April 1986), pp. 69–79.

4. Bruce M. Owen and Steven S. Wildman, *Video Economics* (Harvard University Press, 1992), p. 233.

5. 9 FCC Rcd 4316 (1994), app. C, p. 4.

6. Count of cable companies is from Warren Publishing, January 1995.

7. Owen and Wildman, *Video Economics,* p. 233.

between overbuilt and single-supplier markets in metropolitan statistical areas (see chapter 2). It is possible that both results are correct and that overbuilds affect rates only in more rural areas or that mergers have eliminated situations in which MSAs have significant differences in rates. If overbuilds do lower rates, however, this could provide a powerful incentive for consolidation. Third, a large share of an incumbent cable firm's assets are sunk; therefore, the incumbent may lower rates substantially in the face of a competitive threat. This response may be a powerful deterrent to market entry.[8]

Competition from Telephone Companies

Although virtually every household in the United States has electrical and telephone service, neither the electricity nor the telephone drop lines, as currently configured, could be used to deliver cable television services. The telephone network could, however, be reconfigured.

For more than thirty years, cable had little to fear from telephone companies. Telephone networks were designed to switch low-speed voice circuits, not to deliver broadband television signals. They could not transmit one television signal, much less fifty or more, through paired copper wires. But developments in digital transmission and fiber-optic technologies in the 1970s allowed telephone networks to increase their capacity to transmit digital data streams in response to business demands. The transition from analog to digital transmission and switching followed, particularly after the 1984 AT&T divestiture.

As digital technologies spread, telephone companies began to replace their copper wires with fiber-optic cables. Fiber optics has now been deployed by most telephone companies for many of their connections between switching centers, and the technology is spreading to the feeder lines that radiate from the centers toward the final subscribers. These lines are particularly economical for serving customers who are far from a local switching center. Because they convey signals in digital form, the systems are called digital-loop carrier (DLC) facilities. By the end of the 1980s,

---

8. Leland L. Johnson argues that such a strategy will deter entry of telephone companies as competitors to cable unless the telephone companies can offer services not now available or not potentially available on cable. See *Toward Competition in Cable Television* (MIT Press and the American Enterprise Institute, 1994).

fiber-optic DLC systems were serving 7 percent of all subscriber loops.[9] Since 1989, local telephone companies have more than tripled the number of miles of fiber-optic circuits in their networks.

Fiber to the Home

Because the bandwidth capacity of fiber-optic networks has grown enormously with improvements in technology, telephone companies have realized that as they extend fiber deeper into their networks, they may be able to redesign them to deliver video signals. The bottleneck for video distribution, however, is the distribution plant, the lines that connect each subscriber to the company's feeder lines. This "last mile" of line is still copper in virtually all telephone companies, but that may soon change. At first, telephone companies investigated the possibilities of extending fiber optics all the way to the subscriber. This fiber-to-the-home (FTTH) system would provide sufficient bandwidth to deliver voice, data, and a large number of simultaneous video signals to most subscribers. Bell Atlantic, Southwestern Bell, and GTE have launched trials of the technology.

FTTH technology suffers, however, from one major shortcoming: optical fiber cannot carry enough electrical power to operate all of the electronics required for the network. As a result, a separate metallic line must be strung along the fiber path. In a conventional telephone digital-loop carrier, this power is provided by a connection to the electric utility company with backup battery power along the network at nodal points. But the fiber DLC system converts all signals from optical to radio frequencies at optical network interfaces located along the network's right of way. The signals then move to the subscriber in analog or digital format with the power supplied by the network. This is important because it allows the telephone company to maintain service during power outages. If fiber is extended to the subscriber's premises, standby power will have to be provided either at the premises or through a metallic wire strung from a pedestal along the network. Neither alternative is very attractive.

Fiber to the Curb

An alternative to the all-fiber network is to extend fiber farther than is now the practice in DLC systems but only to a point outside the subscrib-

9. David P. Reed, *Residential Fiber Optic Networks: An Engineering and Economic Analysis* (Boston: Artech House, 1992).

er's home. This point is referred to as a pedestal, a platform underground or on a telephone pole. Here the optical signal is converted into a radio signal for transmission by copper wire or coaxial cable. Such an architecture reduces the cost of electronics required by fiber-to-the-home technology and allows for a more efficient solution to the remote standby powering requirement.

Hybrid Networks

An alternative approach for developing cable-telephony technologies uses a combination of fiber optics and coaxial cable. Cable companies are extending fiber optics along their distribution system, and some telephone companies, particularly Pacific Bell, have investigated the installation of coaxial cable to deliver a mix of narrowband and broadband services. Pacific Bell has begun to build a fiber-optic/coaxial network in major metropolitan areas in California, but recently announced a deferral of plans for all markets except San Francisco. The Pacific Bell architecture involves the transmission of video, data, and voice signals over the same fiber-optic network to remote optical network interfaces from which four coaxial cables would radiate to serve about 500 homes (120 or more for each cable).[10] The cables would drop service off to each household or business much like current cable systems, but the signals would be separated into video analog signals, telephone signals, and data for computers in a network interface unit. Given the bandwidth in this proposed system, Pacific Bell hoped to offer as many as seventy-eight channels of one-way video and a large number of pay-per-view, interactive video, and even video telephony (picture phone) services as well as conventional switched telephone services.

Although some of the technology of the Pacific Bell system is still in development, the company has argued that this hybrid system can be deployed at much less cost than rebuilding a traditional network with DLC and paired copper wires. The coaxial cable system may also provide much greater capacity to subscribers at a lower cost per subscriber than traditional copper wiring. The larger the number of homes passed, the lower the cost. But extending the system to additional homes requires the reservation of more bandwidth on the cable for the interactive video and telephony services. This extension reduces the amount of bandwidth left for

10. These details are available in Pacific Bell's section 214 filing before the Federal Communications Commission. See especially the affidavit filed by Robert G. Harris, "Testimony in Support of Pacific Bell's Section 214 Application to the FCC," December 14, 1993.

cable television services. Apparently, Pacific Bell decided that the best design to service its estimate of prospective demands is 120 homes per coaxial bus. More homes on the bus would reduce services but lower the cost per subscriber; fewer homes would increase costs but allow more services.

The company projected that its fiber-coaxial architecture would result in an outside plant that costs 32 percent less than the current architecture and that the investment required for video services would be only $50 a home.[11] If deployed only as a telephony system, this technology would result in costs 36 percent lower than those for the conventional DLC plant. These assertions translate into an investment of $850 a home for the fiber-coaxial system with video as compared with $1,250 for a fiber-copper DLC system. The historical gross book cost that Pacific Bell reports to the Federal Communications Commission is $900 a line.[12]

Pacific Bell's proposal has not been without controversy. Cable companies have cried foul over its assertion that only $50 of the outside plant investment and $136 of total investment per line will be allocable to video.[13] Regulators will have to allocate the cost of accelerating plant replacement to video services or simply rely on a price cap for telephony so that consumers can be protected from having to support a potential subsidy from telephony to video services.

The installation of advanced ATM (asynchronous transfer mode) switches, high-speed voice-data switches, and remote servers will allow fiber-coaxial networks to deliver a variety of interactive services in addition to cable television and pay-per-view. Most of these networks are still prototypes, as telephone and cable companies experiment with hardware and service packages.[14] In 1995, Bell Atlantic announced that it was withdrawing its requests for FCC authorization of hybrid fiber-coaxial cable systems because it had decided that the fiber-to-the-curb architecture was the better choice for providing the necessary bandwidth for one-way and two-way services.[15] Shortly thereafter the company also announced that it was slow-

11. Harris, "Testimony," p. 8.

12. Federal Communications Commission, *Statistics of Communications Common Carriers, 1992–1993* (1994), pp. 77, 162.

13. See, for example, the affidavit of Leland L. Johnson submitted to the FCC in response to the Pacific Bell section 214 application, file nos. W-P-C 6913-16, February 1994.

14. In late 1994 Time Warner and US West's joint venture began offering various one-way and interactive video services in Orlando, Florida. This service had been delayed because of difficulties in developing the set-top converter through which the consumer interacts with the system.

15. Annie Lindstrom, "Bell Atlantic Puts Video Architecture Plans on Hold," *Telephony,* vol. 228 (May 1, 1995), p. 6.

ing its deployment of these terrestrial wire-based broadband facilities. The switched broadband network operated by telephone companies now appears very much in doubt.

Asynchronous Digital Subscriber Loop

Telephone companies have also investigated using a signal-compression technology over the copper wire distribution loop already connecting the subscriber. Called asynchronous digital subscriber loop, this technology offers the advantage that the companies do not have to make major investments in the network until the subscriber elects the service. Companies must then invest in the central-office switch and the subscriber's premises to initiate the service, perhaps $1,500 or more per subscriber, but there are no other large sunk costs. Thus ADSL could be used where prospective demand for telephone company video services is presumed to be limited. As long as the provisioning cost of each line is less than the network cost per home passed for hybrid fiber-coaxial systems divided by the anticipated penetration of video services over these networks, ADSL may be the better choice. Although its cost is now falling, it remains a high-cost strategy for entering into a business in which the existing cable plant costs much less.

Regulatory Burdens

Under the 1984 Cable Act, telephone companies were prohibited from offering cable television services in their own franchise areas. In 1992 the Federal Communications Commission decided in principle to allow them to offer video dial tone services on a nondiscriminatory, common-carrier basis in order to increase competition in the video marketplace.[16] The companies would not be allowed to have more than an incidental interest in the programming transmitted over their networks, but the commission recommended to Congress that it lift this prohibition subject to certain safeguards. A year later a U.S. district court overturned the ban in a suit by Bell Atlantic.[17] Other telephone companies pursued similar suits, alleging that the prohibition was unconstitutional.

Congress has now passed legislation that overturns the prohibition. If it had not done so, telephone companies would probably have prevailed

---

16. 7 FCC Rcd 5781 (1992), rules sections 63.54–63.58.

17. *Chesapeake and Potomac Telephone Co. of Virginia v United States,* 830 F. Supp. 909, *aff'd,* 42 F.3d 181 (4th Cir. 1994) *cert granted,* 1995 U.S. LEXIS 4273 (June 26, 1995).

in court anyway.[18] Were the telephone companies permitted to offer only common-carrier video dial tone service, however, it is unlikely that they would become full-fledged competitors of cable MSOs. The riskiness of investments in new services or programming requires that there be some probability of very large returns. As common carriers, telephone companies would be unable to participate in the successes of the services. It is likely that they would simply lease infrastructure to other multichannel operators, including the cable company itself. To compete fully with cable companies, multichannel operators must have the latitude to arrange for and even invest in programming, latitude that the 1996 legislation provides.

Competition from Direct Broadcast Satellites

In 1994 two new multichannel video services began broadcasting directly to consumers from two geostationary satellites launched by Hughes Electronics, a subsidiary of General Motors. These services, DirecTV and USSB, use digital signal compression to offer a large number of channels of conventional cable networks and pay-per-view sports events and movies. Consumers may receive this programming by purchasing home reception equipment consisting of an 18-inch dish and the associated electronics required to convert the digital signals to analog signals that can be viewed on a standard television set. In addition, the Primestar satellite system launched by a consortium of cable companies in 1990 is delivering service to 700,000 subscribers, mostly in rural markets. The system requires a 36-inch receiving dish, but it delivers seventy channels of programming for about $30 a month, including the rental of the dish.[19]

It is clear that the sunk costs of DBS market entry are much lower than they are for traditional wire-based cable systems unless the DBS provider also finances the subscribers' receiving equipment. DBS companies are not required to build extensive terrestrial networks before commencing service. The satellites shared by DirecTV and USSB were launched for about $300 million, a small fixed cost for a video service capable of reaching

18. The Supreme Court accepted a petition to hear the Bell Atlantic case in the 1994–95 term.

19. See Frank Beacham, "Primestar Crashes the DBS Party," *TV Technology,* vol. 12 (October 1994), p. 28.

100 million homes immediately with 150 channels or more.[20] The costs of terminal equipment—$700 a home and another $150 to install—are incurred by the subscriber and may prove to be a barrier to developing the service, but the price is expected to decline rapidly with falling prices of electronics components.[21] Another obstacle is the need to install both an antenna for the reception of conventional broadcast signals and a dish to receive the DBS signals because the system has nationwide coverage and cannot retransmit different local broadcast signals to each geographical area.

Leland Johnson and Deborah Castleman have shown that DBS can be competitive with cable if it can enroll 4 million subscribers and the cost of the subscriber's receiving equipment is $300 or less.[22] Their analysis is based on a much higher satellite launch cost than that apparently incurred by the Hughes consortium. With satellite costs of $300 million, the break-even point falls to less than 3 million subscribers. At the margin, however, the cost of adding another subscriber to DBS is simply the amortization of the system's receiving equipment plus marketing expenditures. Once the cost of receivers, including installation, falls to about $500, DBS should render traditional cable television service contestable, assuming that it and cable deliver a similar array of services with equivalent reception quality.

Unlike many terrestrial alternatives to cable, DBS is already available. Subscribers who purchase the requisite equipment can receive one of several packages of cable networks, movies, music, and sports. In this sense, cable is already contestable. DBS lacks only the ability to provide two-way services and local broadcast stations. Cable systems, of course, are also unable to provide two-way, switched video services with their current architecture. Therefore, unless subscribers place a high value on local programming, cable rates will not be able to increase without inducing some

20. This cost is not necessarily sunk because the satellites could be used for services other than DBS if the system proves uneconomical. Canadian cable and broadcast systems and the Canadian government have reacted with alarm at this new competitor, known north of the border as Death Star, whose satellites' footprints cover most of the populous areas of Canada. In 1995 the Canadian Radio-Television and Telecommunications Commission mandated a major increase in Canadian-based cable channels on Canada's cable systems as a (dubious) strategy for fending off the U.S.-owned DirecTV and USSB services.

21. Rich Brown and Harry J. Jessell, "Dishing Up Full-Power DBS," *Broadcasting & Cable*, vol. 124 (March 28, 1994), pp. 48–51; and Beacham, "Primestar Crashes the DBS Party." The DirecTV-USSB equipment was initially manufactured only by RCA, but in mid-1995 Sony also began to manufacture the receivers.

22. Leland L. Johnson and Deborah R. Castleman, *Direct Broadcast Satellites: A Competitive Alternative to Cable Television?* (Santa Monica, Calif.: RAND, 1991), p. 24.

Table 5-1. *Forecasts of Total DBS Subscribers, 1995–99*
Millions

Forecaster	1995	1996	1997	1998	1999
DirecTV	0.85	2.04	5.30	9.55	13.84
Hubbard (aggressive)	0.90	2.34	6.79	13.57	21.04
Hubbard (conservative)	0.85	2.04	5.31	9.55	13.84
EchoStar	1.31	3.24	6.01	9.40	11.82
Paul Kagan (aggressive)	2.99	5.37	7.78	9.72	11.60
Paul Kagan (conservative)	1.07	1.98	2.90	3.82	4.66
Leland Johnson (RAND)	0.79	1.75	4.27	7.32	10.24

Source: Tom Kerver, "Between the Lines," *Cablevision* (November 14, 1994), p. 6.

consumer shift toward DBS. In 1996 two additional DBS services will be available, offering between 90 and 200 channels.[23] Soon we shall have estimates of the extent to which consumers consider the three DBS services as substitutes for cable.[24]

It is still far too early to estimate the effect of DBS on cable rates or services. Industry participants and observers are predicting that subscriptions to the systems will total 4.7 million to 21.0 million by 1999 (table 5-1). But DBS subscriptions will reflect receiver prices, cable rates, DBS services, and cable services. DBS could serve as a strong potential competitor of cable with only a few million subscribers, particularly in rural areas where cable services are far from ubiquitous, operators are far more likely to have systems with small capacities, and the FCC cable-rate regressions have shown the largest effect of competition from overbuilds occurs in these rural areas (see chapter 2).

Competition from Wireless Cable

A third category of competitors to cable is the terrestrial wireless services now generally lumped together under the term *wireless cable.* These ser-

23. Mark Hallinger, "DBS Systems Set to Fly in '96," *TV Technology,* vol. 14 (January 12, 1996), p. 8; and Shira McCarthy, "MCI, News Corp. Launch DBS Plans for New Spectrum," *Telephony,* vol. 230 (January 29, 1996), p. 3.

24. Hollinger, "DBS Systems Set to Fly," p. 8. As of late 1995, Primestar had only 975,000 subscribers because its medium-power satellite had a more limited channel capacity than the other DBS systems. DirecTV, with a higher-powered satellite and smaller receiver dishes, has enrolled about 1 million.

vices transmit multiple video channels through the electromagnetic spectrum from local facilities. They include microwave multichannel multipoint distribution services (MMDS), offering as many as thirty-three channels to subscribers who install an inexpensive microwave receiver, and newer cellular cable services that use the spectrum much more efficiently, providing more channels. Cellular cable, however, is still in initial stages of development.

MMDS systems have been in existence for several decades, but only recently have they been provided access to sufficient electromagnetic spectrum to offer programming that can be compared to cable's. Even today, they must share as many as twenty of their thirty-three channels with the instructional television service. Moreover, MMDS suffers from line-of-sight limitations caused by transmitting from a central terrestrial location over a service area that reflects the earth's curvature and other topographical impediments. But the systems, unlike DBS, can retransmit local broadcast signals.

There are some 200 MMDS systems in operation serving 750,000 subscribers, most of whom are located in the Great Plains states.[25] MMDS is not a major competitor for cable in the largest urban markets, but the introduction of digital signal compression, with its greater carrying capacity, may increase its competitiveness. Such an advance would, however, also increase the cost of home reception equipment, undercutting one of its primary advantages over DBS. Moreover, the regional Bell operating companies, particularly Bell Atlantic, Nynex, and Pacific Telesis, are beginning to invest in MMDS as a transitional strategy to enable them to enter video markets.[26]

An even more intriguing possibility is a cellular form of wireless cable being tested in two boroughs of New York City and in Calgary, Alberta. Signals are distributed by low-power transmission within small cells at 28 GHz so that individual frequencies may be used again and again within a narrow geographic area. At present, cellular cable is designed to offer forty-nine channels of one-way television service at a monthly rate of $30

25. Mark Hallinger, "Wireless Cable Ready for the World," *TV Technology,* vol. 13 (July 1995), pp. 1, 40.

26. The regional Bell operating companies apparently are trying to spread their risk of developing new video services by investing in a variety of technologies. Bell Atlantic and Nynex have invested in CAI, an eastern MMDS operator. Pacific Telesis has announced that it will purchase a wireless company in Southern California. See Jason Meyers, "Pacific Telesis Catches a Ride on the Wireless Cable Wave," *Telephony,* vol. 228 (April 24, 1995), p. 6.

a subscriber, but it is capable of offering more channels and interactive video. Bell Atlantic and Philips have joined a consortium to develop this service throughout North America.

It is too soon to know if terrestrial wireless services will emerge as viable competitors to cable. However, the experiments with cellular wireless cable appear promising, and the new emphasis on market-based allocations for electromagnetic spectrum may lead to far more of the spectrum being available for MMDS systems.[27] These services along with DBS are surely a threat to traditional cable systems and are likely to provide a limit to any market power they could exercise even without regulation.

One-Way Video or the Information Superhighway?

Cable television is currently a one-way video service with only limited two-way capabilities, generally for ordering pay-per-view events. Given the advances in electronics in general and digital signal compression in particular, systems are being developed to deliver vast amounts of one-way video, switched voice and data, and two-way switched video over the same terrestrial network, particularly the various fiber-optic fiber–coaxial cable networks. The development of two-way video capacity opens up a great potential for these networks, albeit in the form of services whose dimensions and public acceptance cannot be clearly predicted. Interactive games, educational services, and shopping are the most prominently mentioned forms that may appear on these networks.

The potential for these services has excited a wave of joint ventures between telephone companies and cable operators. The regional Bell operating companies, in particular, are seeking to break loose from the geographic boundaries in which they have been confined since the 1984 AT&T divestiture. They have entered into numerous joint ventures with cable companies outside their own regions, seeking to transform these one-way networks into two-way full-service operations.[28] None of the ventures is fully operational, but each poses a potential competitive threat to estab-

27. The FCC auctioned three blocks of spectrum for personal communications services in 1994–95.

28. The most prominent of these joint ventures, Bell Atlantic's acquisition of TCI, the country's largest cable operator, was abandoned in the wake of the 1994 FCC cable rulings. However, others such as US West's joint venture with Time-Warner continue to move cautiously forward.

lished local telephone companies and is placing pressure on them to offer their own distributed and switched video services.

It is still an open question whether the march of new technology will induce the construction of more than one two-way broadband (video, voice, and data) network in most communities. Obviously there are economies in having only one such network, but the race to offer new services may lead both the incumbent telephone and cable companies to attempt to convert their networks into full two-way broadband services.

If one-way cable service were the only broadband service demanded by households, two parallel systems would probably not develop. Now that telephone companies are free from the strictures of the 1984 Cable Act, they might build one-way cable systems along their rights of way, but only to distribute the existing cable company's services. The telephone company would simply replace the cable company as a transmission facility.[29] If households want switched two-way video services, the outcome might be different as cable and telephone companies compete to develop successful network architectures and service packages. Because the most effective design of such a system is still very much in doubt, parallel systems could be built in a large number of communities.

Our discussion of switched broadband networks has ignored the wireless services. At this stage in the electronics-communications revolution, wire-based networks appear to be better positioned to offer switched two-way services. The amount of electromagnetic spectrum required to offer two-way video communications would simply be too great, given current technology and spectrum-allocation policies. DBS, in particular, can only offer distributed video; the satellites cannot receive unique broadband transmissions back from thousands or millions of dispersed subscribers. The cellular cable companies might be able to devise a technique of spectrum sharing that allows two-way video communication, but this technology is still in its infancy for even one-way applications.

Effects on Cable System Equities and Acquisition Prices

If multichannel video services were to become a contestable market, one might expect cable franchise values to be pushed toward the reproduction

---

29. This is the outlook offered by Johnson, *Toward Competition in Cable Television.*

cost of assets as new technologies appeared and were shown to be viable.[30] This would be reflected both in cable system sales prices and in the share prices of system operators. As we showed in chapter 4, however, this downward adjustment in values has been modest at best and may be more a response to the strictures of the Cable Act than to the threat of competition.

Ironically, competitive pressures may have actually increased the market value of cable systems. The developments in technology that are creating the possibility of switched broadband networks may portend additional competition from telephone companies, but they may also increase the bidding for existing cable systems' coaxial cable networks. Indeed, this is precisely what happened when Bell Atlantic, US West, and Southwestern Bell began looking for opportunities to upgrade existing cable networks outside their franchise areas.

Conclusion

Is competition possible in multichannel video services? The question barely survives the asking, for competition already exists in the form of direct broadcast satellites and wireless cable. DBS, in particular, looms as a major force, propelled in part by an investment of up to $1 billion by Hughes Electronics. Whether the systems will attract enough customers to put downward pressure on cable subscriptions and rates is not yet clear. However, at a fixed cost of $700 a subscriber that is falling, DBS would appear to be a major competitor for cable, whose plant has cost operators $500 to $700 a subscriber.

The video market is not static. Yesterday's innovations were ESPN, CNN, Arts and Entertainment, and pay-per-view movies and sports. Technology is moving so rapidly that a vast array of new services may soon be available on the same infrastructure that delivers cable television, telephone, or both. Regulation of cable television and telephony formerly served to inhibit each in its attempts to invade the other's domain. The regulation of telephone companies directly protected cable operators, and rate regulation of cable threatened to reduce its ability to compete with telephone companies.

30. The reproduction cost of assets must include the costs associated with negotiating for a franchise, planning the development of the system, arranging for rights-of-way, and building a subscriber base. Thus one would not expect franchise values to be the same as the engineering-based estimates of building the system.

The laws that prevented competition between cable operators and telephone companies have been superseded by the Telecommunications Act of 1996. Cable operators may now offer telephone services, and telephone companies may now offer video services. Whether these local markets will become contestable remains to be seen, but regulation should no longer be a major obstacle.

CHAPTER SIX

Where Do We Go from Here?

T HE cable industry is still subject to some rate regulation.[1] But other forms of multichannel video services may eventually attain a sufficient market presence to induce the repeal of rate regulation altogether. Because no one knows how rapidly these new rivals will enroll subscribers, cable rate regulation, like rent control or natural gas regulation, is likely to remain in some form despite its potential for retarding investment, slowing the adoption of new technologies, and eroding the quality of service from what it might have been without regulation.

The Cable Television Consumer Protection and Competition Act of 1992 created something of a natural economic experiment. Some franchises were spared mandatory rate regulation because they met the criteria for being in a market with effective competition. Other franchises were not so lucky. As improvements in technology occur, cable subscribers in all franchises will benefit from new services. But the rate of investment and adoption of the technologies would likely have been slower in the regulated franchises. In the short run the adverse effects of rate regulation might not have been perceptible. But over time, particularly if new competition had not quickly emerged, differences in the quality of service would have become apparent if Congress had not moved to deregulate most rates by 1999. In the interim the FCC could claim that it has saved most consumers from 10 to 17 percent on basic cable service. Unfortunately, because the worst effects of price controls accumulate slowly, there will be little evidence of the effect of the 1992 act on cable service quality and, as a result, little ammunition for those seeking to oppose the next lurch toward regulation if it occurs. It is imperative therefore that competition develop quickly so as not to create the political environment for a return to full rate regulation.

---

1. The Telecommunications Act of 1996 repealed all upper-tier rate regulation. Small cable operators are exempted from all rate regulation, and other cable operators will be freed from rate regulation if a telephone company enters their franchise area with a comparable video service. Otherwise, only basic rates are regulated after March 31, 1999.

Competition as a Substitute for Rate Regulation

Competition for cable services from telephone companies, direct broadcast satellite systems, wireless cable, and other sources should have a double benefit. Competitors will surely reduce consumer prices, spur innovation and adaptation of new technologies, and offer subscribers a wider array of choices. Just how quickly this competition will develop is still unknown.

Liberalization of Telephone Company Market Entry

The legislative impediment to telephone company entry into local video distribution has now been removed by the Telecommunications Act of 1996. The 1984 Cable Act had prohibited a local telephone company from owning interests in programming offered over its network. As a result, telephone companies were relegated by statute to offering common-carriage services or simple video dial tone. The 1996 act repeals this prohibition and allows the companies to enter in one of two ways.[2]

First, a local telephone company may own and operate a video distribution system, either wireless or cable, subject largely to the same rules applicable to other such wireless or cable services under the Communications Act of 1934. The clear intent of Congress is to allow telephone companies to own competing distribution systems; cross-ownership between a local telephone company and an existing video service is limited to 10 percent.[3] To further facilitate telephone entry, the 1996 act removes the regulatory burdens of section 214, heretofore imposed on telephone company video dial-tone services.[4]

Second, a local telephone company may avoid some of the regulatory burdens of title III and title VI of the Telecommunications Act by offering video services as a common carrier on an "open video system." A local telephone company choosing this option must offer video channels to other providers and may select the programming for no more than one-third of its total channels if demand exceeds capacity. To qualify for this

---

2. Telecommunications Act of 1996, sections 651, 652, and 653. Because this act amends the Communications Act of 1934, all references are formally to the 1934 act (47 U.S.C. 151*et.seq.*)

3. Sections 652(a), (b), and (c). Paradoxically, section 652 (d) provides exemptions to the cross-ownership restrictions for cable systems in rural areas, precisely the systems most likely to have any form of market power. See chapter 2.

4. Communications Act of 1934, section 651 (c).

status, and the reduced regulatory burdens, however, the local telephone company must obtain FCC certification.[5]

Telephone company entry into video services creates another policy problem—how to avoid cross-subsidies. As long as the telephone companies are regulated at the state or federal level on the basis of their costs of providing ordinary switched voice and data services, they have an incentive to hide some of the costs of entering the video market in the cost of their traditional, regulated activities.[6] The obvious solution is to substitute a form of rate-cap regulation for the cost-based form, but many state regulators are reluctant to allow telephone companies this freedom potentially to unleash the forces of telephone-rate rebalancing.[7] Thus state regulators are major roadblocks to the development of video competition or, more generally, the information superhighway.

At this juncture, no telephone company in the United States (or in any other country, for that matter) offers serious video competition for cable companies.[8] We cannot know whether this reflects technical problems in developing fiber-optic/coaxial cable networks with the appropriate consumer interfaces, the difficulty in justifying market entry against entrenched incumbents with large sunk costs, or regulators' intransigence in altering the regulatory environment to allow entry without creating an endless battle over cross-subsidies and cost allocations. Congress has now moved to help resolve the dilemma, however, by removing many of the formal barriers to telephone company entry into video service. We may soon obtain an answer to the question of whether there will be one wire or two competing for subscribers.

Wireless Technologies

Multichannel video competition may develop from a second wire to the home or from wireless technologies, including multichannel multipoint

5. Communications Act of 1934, section 653.

6. Even the FCC's rate cap regulation of local-exchange companies has a cost-based component. Carriers are permitted to keep only a portion of their profits above a target rate of return.

7. State regulation results in telephone rates that often do not reflect costs, with long-distance rates and urban local-access rates generally subsidizing flat-rate residential service in suburban and rural locations. Limited attempts at state regulatory reform have had remarkably little effect on telephone rate structures. Moreover, few state regulators are willing to establish rate chaps without some form of revenue sharing that would dilute the protections against cross-subsidies. See Robert W. Crandall and Leonard Waverman, *Talk Is Cheap: The Promise of Regulatory Reform in North American Communications* (Brookings, 1996).

8. There are some pilot programs, but no telephone company has begun to offer cable television service to a large share of its subscribers.

distribution services, cellular cable, and direct broadcast satellites. At this juncture, cellular cable technology is experimental and not likely to develop into a full-fledged competitor of traditional cable until its technical and economic viability are proven. The other two options are already in commercial operation.

MMDS or other terrestrial wireless services could become much more formidable competitors of cable if they could reach more homes with a greater variety of programming. MMDS has to be allocated more spectrum before it can offer more than its current thirty channels of full-time or part-time programming. Alternatively, MMDS operators will have to employ new technologies for digital signal compression to expand their capacity to 100 channels or more. MMDS does not require a distribution network of wires, poles, and conduits or other barriers to market entry, so greater potential channel capacity could induce immediate entry. Because MMDS services have a limited geographic reach, they can offer viewers a variety of local broadcast signals in addition to national cable networks and premium services if they have sufficient capacity. Given the FCC's movement toward using auctions to allocate spectrum, we see no reason why potential MMDS companies should not be invited to bid for unused spectrum space or even to buy it away from lower-valued uses. Recently the Bell companies have begun to invest in MMDS rather than build expensive fiber-coaxial cable networks. This suggests that at least some market participants are optimistic about the future of MMDS as a video-distribution technology.

Three direct broadcast satellites are serving major population centers in the United States. With up to 170 channels, these systems can offer a large array of national or international programming. Before we can determine whether subscribers consider DBS a substitute for cable, they will need time to make their choices. Time is also required to see whether enough subscribers will switch from cable to DBS if cable systems were to exert monopoly power and raise their rates. Public policy can do little to affect these decisions now that the courts have overturned the regulations imposed on DBS systems in the 1992 Cable Act. Similar manditory signal-carriage requirements imposed on cable systems should also be reexamined, but Congress has been unwilling to do so.

Coping with Regulation

By 1999 the regulation of cable rates for all but a basic tier will have disappeared, unless Congress changes its mind once again. Nevertheless, a great deal of cable regulation remains. Rates for equipment rentals are still regulated. Must-carry provisions remain for broadcast signals. There are limits on the total number of cable subscribers that a single MSO may serve. There are limits on the number of channels that a cable operator may devote to programming in which the operator has a financial interest. If Congress is willing to deregulate most rates, presumably because it observes increasing competition in the video marketplace, why has it not moved to clear the landscape of all of this regulatory underbrush?

The Increasing Complexity of the Service

We are now about to reap the benefits of digital signal compression that began with DirecTV. DBS offers about 170 channels of service, and fiber-optic/coaxial cable service is about to expand to 500 or more. If cable television simply multiplies the number of its one-way channels by five or six, it will find itself scrambling to discover enough attractive programming to offer. Regulated basic service may occupy only a small share of these channels. What if a cable system owner, following service expansion, objects to its regulated basic rates and asks for a cost-of-service ratemaking proceeding? How do regulators allocate the costs of service of a system that has grown to such dimensions? Given the impossibility of allocating the joint costs of the distribution network, would rates be set in an efficient fashion?[9] If so, basic service rates might have the highest markup over marginal cost, since basic service is likely to have the lowest price elasticity of demand. In the 1992 act Congress wanted precisely the opposite form of pricing: low basic rates for everyone. This vision of universal service is similar to the one that has distorted telephone rates so badly, limited entry into local telephone service, and reduced economic welfare in the United States by as much as $30 billion a year because it must be financed from super-competitive long-distance rates.[10]

Even more perplexing to regulators will be problems stemming from the development of switched, two-way voice and video services. Cablevision has begun to offer telephone service from its Long Island cable systems. Time Warner, for example, is poised to enter the telephone market in

9. This approach was developed by Frank Ramsey nearly seventy years ago. See William J. Baumol and David F. Bradford, "Optimal Departures from Marginal Cost Pricing," *American Economic Review,* vol. 60 (June 1970), pp. 265–83.

10. See Robert W. Crandall, *After the Break Up: U.S. Telecommunications in a More Competitive Era* (Brookings, 1991), and its citations of earlier literature. For more recent estimates, see Crandall and Waverman, *Talk Is Cheap.*

Rochester, New York, and is developing a much more sophisticated two-way network in Orlando, Florida. All major cable companies are attempting alliances with MCI, AT&T, and other telephone carriers to develop wireless applications using the personal communications system spectrum auctioned in 1995. As the cable networks evolve into this combination of traditional cable service and switched services, and if every cable system can continue to request a cost-of-service regulatory proceeding, how will regulators sort out the costs of basic cable service from myriad other one-way and new two-way switched services?

The FCC's experience in attempting to allocate AT&T's costs between competitive and monopoly services in the 1960s and 1970s was so unsatisfactory that it was essentially forced to abandon the quest. By the middle of the 1980s the commission was induced to turn to rate regulation rather than cost-of-service regulation, in part because of its earlier experience. In the 1990s the commission is once again facing demands to allocate costs of regulated telephone companies seeking to enter the video market. Cable companies have complained that attempts by Pacific Bell and Bell Atlantic to extend their network capabilities to video services will subsidize video services from regulated telephone services. The commission will soon be faced with similar complaints from telephone companies as cable systems begin to provide switched voice and data services over retrofitted cable systems.

Effects of Cable Regulation on New Services

We have analyzed the importance of improvements in cable television service quality since 1986. We are convinced that the sharp expansion in the number and diversity of services contributed strongly to consumer welfare even after accounting for the increases in real subscriber rates. Cable now faces prospects of even more dramatic expansion of capacity because of digital-compression technologies moving toward commercialization. Unfortunately, continuing the current regulatory regime, if only for basic service, may create disincentives to invest in new programming. Even though the 1996 Act will deregulate all upper-tier services by 1999, the FCC's regulatory apparatus remains in place. Thus the threat of yet another bout of rate regulation hangs over the industry, particularly if political control of Congress changes once again.

Populist demands for affordable universal service could therefore suppress programming innovations. Few observers in 1980 would have dreamed that access to scores of video channels would be labeled basic service, much less that such service would be subject to federal rate regulation.[11] Today's exotic, advanced tiers of programming could easily become tomorrow's basic service, subject to rate controls and assurances of universal access. Unfortunately, there is nothing that Congress can do to promise investors that it will not respond to these political pressures in two or three years, particularly in light of its refusal to enact total deregulation.

Conclusion

The expanding number and diversity of channels available to cable subscribers have much improved their welfare. These expansions had their genesis in 1977–79 when the courts and the FCC released the draconian restrictions that the commission had imposed on all subscription television systems, including cable. Between 1984 and 1992, the era of cable rate deregulation, the net improvement in consumer welfare was more than $6 billion a year after deducting for the rising cable rates that fed the political charge for reregulation.

We cannot rule out the possibility that cable had monopoly power in 1984–92 and still may have it. Such power may be limited in major urban areas because theaters, a large number of broadcast stations, video rentals, live events, and other diversions are readily available (we did not find any evidence that competition resulting from cable franchise overlaps in metropolitan statistical areas increased or decreased subscriber rates). However, even if substantial monopoly power exists, unregulated power may generate economic results superior to those obtainable under rate regulation. The very large increases in consumer welfare during the 1984–92 deregulation should show legislators and regulators that regulating the rates that can be charged on a service as differentiated and changing as cable television is counterproductive.

The revival in regulation reduced rates for basic cable service, which in turn led to a decrease of perhaps 15 to 20 percent in the real price of cable systems in recent acquisitions. Together these results suggest a short-term transfer of wealth from cable owners to cable subscribers, surely one of the goals of those supporting regulation. Congress has now recognized that imposing rate regulation runs the risk of reducing investments in cable sys-

11. The late 1970s and 1980s were, after all, a period of deregulation for airlines, trucking, air cargo, oil, and natural gas.

tem improvements and new program offerings. Although upper tiers of cable service are no longer subject to regulation, neither were basic services in 1990 or 1991. Cable owners, like investors in housing in rent-controlled areas, must be aware that new services today become candidates for regulation as old services tomorrow.

We hope that politicians and regulators will heed our advice to rely more on competition than on regulation in this rapidly changing sector. All over the world, consortia are forming to compete in bringing video programming through broadcast channels, satellites, cable systems, and telephone networks. In the United States this potential competition is more advanced than in most other countries, but many regulatory obstacles prevented full exploitation of the new technologies that have developed over the past decade.[12] The 1996 act has now removed many of these obstacles.

Traditional economic regulation of airlines, trucking, telephone, and electricity has been discredited as costing the U.S. economy billions of dollars a year, in no small part because regulation inhibited innovation in technology and service options. Surely, attempting to regulate cable television will be even more damaging, given the rate of technical progress in distributing video signals and the intangible nature of its highly differentiated service. Regulators cannot know where the technology is carrying us, nor can they possibly know what the cost of any new service is or will be. Some alternative to regulation must be found. We believe that it is simply competition.

12. An exception to the U.S. lead may be Australia, where Optus Vision (a consortium of Australia's second telephone company, a U.S. cable company, and two broadcasters) is preparing to spend $3 billion (Australian) to offer pay television and cable services in competition with Telstra, the principal Australian telephone carrier. Telstra is investing $710 million (Australian) to build a fiber-optic/coaxial cable video network in Australia's largest cities. Glenda Korporaal, "Vision Splendid: How Optus Plans to Outgrow Telecom," *Financial Review,* October 14, 1994.

APPENDIX A

Estimation of Demand for Cable
Television Based on Cable System Data

EVEN though cable television is one of the fastest growing industries in the United States, relatively few economic studies of consumer demand for cable services have been published. In this appendix we discuss some of the difficulties in measuring that demand, particularly using data aggregated by cable system. For example, one of the primary obstacles is to distinguish consumer aversion to higher prices from consumer preferences for higher quality of service, which is one of the principal objectives of our study. Only by understanding the trade-offs between price and quality can we measure whether improvements in service in the past decade have compensated consumers for higher cable bills. This appendix also presents an example of a demand model based on data aggregated at the level of the cable system and discusses some of the difficulties encountered with the model. Finally, we describe a method of measuring the change in post-1986 system characteristics for operators that had been previously regulated relative to those that had not.

Difficulties in Measuring Demand

Studies of the demand for cable services in recent years have encountered some or all of the following difficulties: identifying demand; measuring own-price effects, price effects of other goods and services, quality of cable service, the effect of bundling cable services, and the effect of demographic factors; and obtaining the relevant current data.

Identification of Demand

The price of cable services is determined by demand and supply conditions and is thus endogenous to both. Without accounting for the endogeneity, an equation that specifies market quantity as a function of market price—the number of cable subscribers as a function of basic cable fees—may equally well incorporate information about demand and supply conditions. The sensitivity of quantity to price in such an equation cannot unambiguously be attributed to either demand or supply. Sorting out information about demand relationships from information about supply conditions is part of the identification problem in measuring demand relationships with market data.

There are three broad ways to solve the identification problem when estimating demand equations: (1) estimating reduced-form equations that omit endogenous variables such as price; (2) estimating structural equations that account for the simultaneity of price and other factors by using exogenous instruments to predict those endogenous variables; and (3) using data for which price is actually exogenous.

Even if demand and supply conditions in a market are complex, endogenous variables can always be estimated as a function of all independent variables in the market. Thus basic cable fees, while dependent on both demand and supply, can be estimated with reduced-form equations as a function of exogenous factors such as the geographic and demographic characteristics of a community. Because the endogenous variables incorporate information about market equilibrium, the resulting equations cannot be unambiguously labeled as either demand or supply equations. These equations are extremely useful if the information sought is the sensitivity of an endogenous variable to an exogenous variable. For example, reduced-form equations have been successfully estimated for the sensitivity of basic cable fees to the number of local broadcast signals and to various communitywide demographic characteristics.[1] Reduced-form equations, however, are not useful for our study, whose purpose is to estimate the sensitivity of one endogenous variable—demand as measured by the number of subscribers or the decision to subscribe to two other potentially endogenous variables—price and quality of service.

Structural demand equations can be estimated as long as the endogeneity of variables is properly taken into account. The most common ap-

1. For sensitivity to broadcast signals, see Robert W. Crandall, "Regulation, Competition, and Cable Performance," appended to TCI Comments in MM Docket no. 90-4, April 6, 1990; James N. Dertouzos and Steven S. Wildman, "Competitive Effects of Broadcast Signals on Cable," paper prepared for the National Cable Television Association, March 1990; and Mark M. Bykowsky and Tim Sloan, "Competitive Effects of Broadcast Signals on the Price of Basic Service," Office of Policy Analysis and Development Staff Paper, National Telecommunications and Information Administration, April 6, 1990.

For communitywide characteristics, see John R. Woodbury and Kenneth C. Baseman, "Assessing the Effect of Rate Deregulation on Cable Subscribers," conference paper, American Enterprise Institute, Washington, October 10, 1990.

proach is to use instrumental variable techniques. Demand equations for basic cable services have been estimated using instrumental variable techniques applied to cable system data.[2] These studies have estimated demand for basic cable services as a function of price and other factors. From these studies have emerged measures of the own-price elasticity of demand ranging from -1.0 to -2.3.[3]

A third approach to estimating demand equations is to use data for which prices, quality, and other variables that influence demand are actually exogenous. Household-level data meet these conditions.[4] The decision of a household to subscribe to cable is influenced by price and quality. Price and quality of cable service are largely independent of the subscription decision of an individual household, but they are dependent on the aggregate responses of all or a large group of households within in a system. Recent studies of cable demand have primarily been conducted at the level of the cable system. Appendix B presents our estimation of cable demand based on household-level data.

Measurement of Own-Price Effects

Even among studies that use instrumental variable techniques with cable system data, measures of the price sensitivity of demand are often unre-

2. See Robert W. Crandall, "Elasticity of Demand for Cable Service and the Effect of Broadcast Signals on Cable Prices," Appended to TCI comments in MM Docket no. 90-4, April 16, 1990; John W. Mayo and Yasuji Otsuka, "Demand, Pricing, and Regulation: Evidence from the Cable TV Industry," *RAND Journal of Economics*, vol. 22 (Autumn 1991), pp. 396–410; Robert N. Rubinovitz, "Market Power and Price Increases for Basic Cable Service since Deregulation," *RAND Journal of Economics*, vol. 24 (Spring 1993), pp. 1–18; Richard O. Beil Jr. and others, "Competition and the Price of Municipal Cable Television Services: An Empirical Study," *Journal of Regulatory Economics*, vol. 5 (December 1993), pp. 401–15; and Tasneem Chipty, "Horizontal Integration for Bargaining Power: Evidence from the Cable Television Industry," *Journal of Economics and Management Strategy*, vol. 4 (Summer 1995).

3. Mayo and Otsuka, "Demand, Pricing, and Regulation," have estimates showing relatively inelastic demand for basic cable with an average value of the own-price elasticity of -1.0. Crandall has estimates showing considerably more elastic demand for basic cable with a value of the own-price elasticity as high as -2.3.

4. The most recent published study of household demand for cable television appears to be Michael. O. Wirth and Harry Bloch, "Household-Level Demand for Cable Television: A Probit Analysis," *Journal of Media Economics*, vol. 2 (Fall 1989), pp. 21–34. This study, however, is based on 1984 data and does not account for price or quality of cable services. Earlier studies of household demand for cable services include Kent G. Webb, *The Economics of Cable Television* (Lexington, Mass.: Lexington Books, 1983), pp. 67–100; and Janay Collins, Joey Reagan, and John D. Abel, "Predicting Cable Subscribership: Local Factors," *Journal of Broadcasting*, vol. 27 (Spring 1983), pp. 177–83.

liable. One reason is the lack of robustness among different instrument sets. Complications also arise from the aggregation and measurement of prices. Most studies use systemwide data and published list prices for cable services. But because cable operators often employ promotional activities, discounts, and other marketing means to attract subscribers, many consumers do not pay the full price.[5] Most studies of cable demand have not been able to measure the actual price paid by subscribers and consequently may not have been able to measure accurately their price sensitivity. Inaccurate price measurement is often associated with inaccurate quality measurement because prices vary with the quality of service within a cable system. Even across cable systems, rates and quality are strongly correlated. For example, between 1982 and 1993, national average real prices for basic service and the average channel capacity of cable systems increased almost in lockstep; the correlation of these annual series is more than 0.99.[6]

The aggregation and measurement of other variables such as income and demographic characteristics that influence demand complicate the measurement of price sensitivity. These factors, which are necessarily aggregated with system-level data, may distort measurement of both their direct effect on demand and the price effect on demand.

Consumers' preference for quality and aversion to high prices are reflected in cross-sectional data. The correlation between price of basic service and the quality of service is positive, but not as dramatically high, on a cross-sectional basis. The quality of programming as measured by either the number of basic satellite channels, system capacity, or number of broadcast and satellite channels on the basic tier, is positively correlated with the list price of basic service for a sample of 488 cable systems in 1992 (table A-1). As the prices and quality of cable service have increased together, demand studies that measure only the effect of price confound consumer aversion to higher prices with consumer attraction to higher quality. The result is likely to understate consumer sensitivity to either price or quality.

Measurement of Price Effects of Other Goods and Services

The demand for cable service may be influenced by the prices of other cable services, home video services, home entertainment services or prod-

5. List prices may also be based on information from one date while data on the number of subscribers may be based on information from a different date.

6. Based on annual data from Paul Kagan Associates, *Kagan Media Index* (February 26, 1993), p. 2; (April 23, 1993), p. 2; (August 27, 1993), p. 3. The price series was deflated by the CPI-U.

Table A-1. *Correlation between Price and Quality of Basic Cable Television Service, 1992*

Characteristic	Price of basic service	Number of basic satellite channels	System capacity	Number of broadcast and satellite channels on basic tier
Price of basic service	1.000	0.325	0.284	0.310
Number of basic satellite channels	0.325	1.000	0.575	0.907
System capacity	0.284	0.575	1.000	0.632
Number of broadcast and satellite channels on basic tier	0.310	0.907	0.632	1.000

Source: Authors' calculations based on a sample of 488 cable systems in 1992 from Warren Publishing, *Television and Cable Factbook* (1993).

ucts, and away-from-home services. Reliable time-series data on prices for these goods and services are difficult to find; reliable cross-section data that would correspond to most of studies of demand for cable services do not exist. Consequently, the prices of potentially competing services are typically omitted variables in the specification of the demand for cable services.[7]

Measurement of the Quality of Cable Service

The demand for cable television, like the demand for any service, is likely to be strongly influenced by the quality of the service. As discussed in chapter 2, the quality of cable service varies substantially from system to system. Even if all other factors in two systems were identical, demand patterns would likely still differ.

Until the past few years, few studies of the demand for cable television have distinguished the influence of cable-only networks on the quality of service. Studies of the demand for cable services from the 1960s and early 1970s predate the development of cable networks.[8] Studies based on data from the late 1970s and early 1980s commingled cable networks with in-

---

7. The direction of the bias on parameter estimates from the omission of several unobserved variables in a multiple regression model is indeterminate.

8. William S. Comanor and Bridger M. Mitchell, "Cable Television and the Impact of Regulation," *Bell Journal of Economics and Management Science,* vol. 2 (Spring 1971), pp. 154–212; Rolla Edward Park, "Prospects for Cable in the 100 Largest Television Markets," *Bell Journal of Economics and Management Science,* vol. 3 (Spring 1972), pp. 130–50; and Roger G. Noll, Merton J. Peck, and John J. McGowan, *Economic Aspects of Television Regulation* (Brookings, 1973).

dependent broadcast stations. For example, John Mayo and Yasuji Otsuka, working with 1982 data, and Patricia Pacey and Kent Webb, working with 1979 data, focus on the cable carriage of broadcast networks and
duplicate signals.[9] One explanation for the lack of attention given cable
networks in earlier research is that large numbers of cable networks began
to emerge only in the early 1980s. The quality of cable service has also
improved consistently and rapidly. Cable viewers today have access to
more channels and greater diversity of programming than ever before. In
many cases networks are spending increasing sums to improve the quality
of programming.

Measurement of the Effect of Bundling Cable Services

Households often subscribe to bundles of cable services that may include basic programming services, premium services, and equipment rentals. Subscription to a basic service is usually required to obtain other cable
services. Many studies examine cable demand for basic programming only,
without accounting for the simultaneous demand for other services.[10] The
determination of price and quality of basic programming services likely
depends on the demand for these related services.

Measurement of the Effect of Demographic Factors

Household income, size, age distribution, and other demographic characteristics also influence decisions to subscribe to cable. Many studies of
the demand for cable services adjust for various demographic factors, but
the factors are usually measured as distributional statistics for large populations based on county-level data that often do not correspond to cable
system boundaries.[11]

Even if county data corresponded exactly to cable system data, inter-
preting the effect on cable penetration of the change in a distributional
statistic, such as the mean county income, is hampered by problems of

9. Mayo and Otsuka, "Demand, Pricing, and Regulation"; Patricia L. Pacey, "Cable
Television in a Less Regulated Market," *Journal of Industrial Economics,* vol. 34 (September
1985), pp. 81–91; and Webb, *Economics of Cable Television.*

10. For a notable exception, see Mayo and Otsuka, "Demand, Pricing, and Regulation."

11. In addition, the dates of the demographic data measurement often do not correspond
exactly to the dates of the cable service information. Consequently, there is a problem of
whether the sample statistics measured for a county at one date correspond to sample
statistics for the cable system at the time cable system information is measured.

aggregation. Under certain conditions changes in these statistics can be interpreted unambiguously for their likely effect on demand. These conditions, however, are not always met. For example, if income were to increase in households that already subscribe to cable but not in households that do not subscribe, measures of county income may increase without any likely effect on cable subscription patterns of individual households. Alternatively, the median or the mean county income may show no change, yet income may increase for the lower quartile of households and decrease for the upper quartile. The aggregate statistic would predict no change in cable subscription patterns, but more disaggregated information might.

Currency of Data

Finally, most published studies of the demand for cable services are based on data that are no longer valid in this rapidly changing market. Chipty's study using 1991 data is the most recent published paper.[12] Other published studies use earlier data. Of course, with the rapid changes in the access to new video technologies and with the imposition of new federal regulations on the cable industry, our study is likely to be dated as well. But the effect of new technologies on demand for cable is likely to have an unambiguous effect: demand will become more price sensitive with increased competition.

A Measure of Welfare Change over Time for Log Linear Aggregated Demand Models

It is possible to measure welfare changes based on aggregate demand for cable services at the system level.[13] In what follows we give an example of how to define welfare changes from the aggregate demand for a cable system in response to changes in basic cable prices and quality. We assume that the communities served by the cable systems have an indirect welfare function that can be expressed as

$$u^{lt} = v(p_b^{lt}, p_I^t, y^{lt}, q^{lt}, Z^{lt}),$$

---

12. Chipty, "Horizontal Integration for Bargaining Power."

13. For other examples of attempts to measure the economic welfare associated with cable services, see Woodbury and Baseman, "Assessing the Effect of Rate Deregulation"; and Richard O. Beil Jr. and others, "Competition and the Price of Municipal Cable Television Services: An Empirical Study," *Journal of Regulatory Economics,* vol. 6 (1993), pp. 401–15.

where u^{lt} is the measure of welfare for the community at location l at time t;[14] v is an indirect utility function with usual properties; p_b^{lt} is the monthly basic cable prices at location l at time t; p_t^i is the index of other prices at time t, assumed to be invariant to location l;[15] y^{lt} is the median household monthly income at location l at time t; q^{lt} is the quality of cable services as measured by the number of satellite channels at location l at time t; and Z^{lt} is a matrix of other factors influencing demand at location l at time t.

Let demand for cable be represented by a log linear function:

(A.1) $\ln x^{lt} = \alpha \ln p^{lt} + \delta \ln y^{lt} + \beta \ln q^{lt} + Z^{lt}\Gamma,$

where x^{lt} is the number of households subscribing to basic cable services at location l at time t; and p^{lt} is the monthly basic cable prices at location l at time t normalized by the price index p_t^i. The specific form of the indirect utility function corresponding to equation (A.1) with cable prices normalized by the price index is

(A.2) $u^{lt} = v(p^{lt}, y^{lt}, q^{lt}, Z^{lt}) = -[\exp(Z^{lt}\Gamma)](q^{lt})^\beta \, p^{lt(1+\alpha)}(1 + \alpha)^{-1}$
$$+ (y^{lt})^{1-\delta}(1-\delta)^{-1},$$
and the corresponding expenditure function is

(A.3) $E(p^{lt}, u^{lt}, q^{lt}, Z^{lt}) = [(1 - \delta)(u^{lt} + [\exp(Z^{lt}\Gamma)](q^{lt})^\beta p^{lt(1+\alpha)}$
$$(1 + \alpha)^{-1})]^{1/(1-\delta)}.$$

The expenditure function evaluated with different values of price and quality of service, observed at a different time, such as τ, is

(A.4) $E(p^{l\tau}, u^{l\tau}, q^{l\tau}, Z^{l\tau}) = [(1 - d)(u^{l\tau} + [\exp(Z^{l\tau}\Gamma)](q^{l\tau})^\beta \, p^{l\tau(1+\alpha)}$
$$(1 + \alpha)^{-1})]^{1/(1-\delta)}.$$

Compensating variation is the minimum change in expenditures required to keep the community as well off under conditions at time τ as under conditions at time t. The compensating variation function to make the commu-

---

14. Of course, u^{lt} is only an aggregate measure of welfare. It does not reflect variations within the community such as those in household preferences or variations in household characteristics such as income. Consequently, an aggregate measure of welfare, such as u^{lt}, may change in one direction in response to changes in cable system prices and quality of service while many households within the community may have welfare changes in the opposite direction.

15. Regional variations in other prices are not observable. Factors influencing any local prices may be reflected in the matrix Z^{lt}.

nity as well off under price and quality combination (p^h, q^h) as under (p^{lt}, q^{lt}) is[16]

(A.5) $CV(p^{lt}, p^h, q^{lt}, q^h, Z^{lt}, u^{lt})$

$$= E(p^h, u^{lt}, q^h, Z^{lt}) - E(p^{lt}, u^{lt}, q^{lt}, Z^{lt})$$

$$= [(1-\delta)(1 + \alpha)^{-1}y^{lt(-\delta)} \{x'[\bullet] \ (p^h)$$

$$- [x^{lt}(p^{lt})]\} + (y^{lt})^{1-\delta}]^{1/(1-\delta)} - y^{lt},$$

where $x[\bullet] = q^{h\beta} p^{h\alpha} y^{lt\delta} \exp(Z^{lt}\Gamma)$.

We used equation A.5 to measure welfare changes for communities between 1984 and 1990 based on parameter estimates from Robert Rubinovitz.[17] At the mean values of the variables in Rubinovitz's sample, the compensating variation is $5.99 per month per household.[18] This estimated compensating variation applies to all households, not just those subscribing to cable. That is, households in 1990 would be willing to pay an average of $5.99 a month to avoid the combination of cable quality and price that had been available in 1984.[19]

Our estimated value of compensating variation suggests that households were much better off with cable service options in 1990 than with those of 1984. This single-point estimate may mask substantial variation in welfare changes among communities and even among different households within a community. There are at least three possible sources of variation. First, the measure is constructed from several parameters in equation A.5 that are estimated by standard econometric techniques. The covariance structure of these estimates leads to a parametric error structure in the estimate of compensating variation. Second, the reported estimate of compensating variation is evaluated at the mean value of variables in the sample. A different estimate of compensating variation would derive from other values of the sample. Third, it is possible that different parameter values would hold for different subsamples of households or communities.

16. For a derivation of compensating variation for a log linear demand function, see Jerry A. Hausman, "Exact Consumer's Surplus and Deadweight Loss," *American Economic Review* (September 1981), pp. 662–76.

17. Rubinovitz, "Market Power and Price Increases for Basic Cable Service."

18. In 1992 dollars adjusted by the CPI-U.

19. This result is paradoxical given that Rubinovitz finds that, holding quality and other factors constant, cable prices were 18 percent higher in 1990 than in 1984. Households, however, valued the expanded 1990 cable services even more than the increase in price, whatever its causes.

Differences in Cable Characteristics between Regulated and Unregulated Franchises

Our analysis of the differences in service and price characteristics between those cable franchises subject to regulation and those not subject to regulation in 1986 is based on data from a recent random sample of cable franchises collected by the FCC.[20] Table A-2 presents summary statistics of geographic and cable service characteristics for franchises offering cable service in 1986.

To isolate the possible effect of regulation on cable characteristics, we estimated the 1986 cable characteristics with simple reduced-form equations as functions of observed exogenous variables over a cross-section of cable franchises.[21] Our parameter estimates are presented in table A-3. For all of the 1986 cable characteristics that we examined—basic price and number of cable channels, basic cable channels, basic satellite networks, and local broadcast channels offered—we found no effect of the presence of cable regulation in the cross-sectional comparison of cable franchises.

Cable characteristics vary substantially across franchises, and the set of exogenous variables that we examined in the cross-sectional reduced-form equations of table A-3 does not fully account for the variation of any of the 1986 cable characteristics, particularly basic fees. It is possible that an effect of regulation would be observable only in terms of changes in characteristics after regulation. We constructed two-stage least-squares models to estimate 1992 cable franchise characteristics as functions of 1986 characteristics and the set of exogenous variables. The instruments are all of the exogenous variables from table A-3. Table A-4 presents the estimated parameters for these models of 1992 cable franchise characteristics.

Cable operators that were subject to rate regulation in 1986 are projected by the model to raise basic fees by approximately 5 percent more than other cable operators by 1992. The regulated operators were also expected to increase their number of basic satellite networks by 10 percent more than other operators. There are, however, no significant differences in the total number of cable channels, basic service channels, or local broadcast stations offered in 1992.

20. Federal Communications Commission, "FCC Cable TV Rate Survey Database: Structure of Database and Explanatory Notes," in MM Docket no. 92-266, March 30, 1994.
21. We assumed that the presence of regulation in 1986 was exogenously determined.

Table A-2. *Summary Statistics for FCC Random Sample of Franchises Operating in 1986*

Variable	Definition	Number of observations	Mean	Standard deviation	Minimum	Maximum
LSAT86	Log of the number of satellite channels offered on all tiers of basic service in 1986	164	2.26548	0.59639	0.69315	3.33220
LTCHAN86	Log of the total number of channels offered for any type of service in 1986	167	3.18357	0.42416	1.94591	4.12713
LTBAS86	Log of the total number of channels offered on all tiers of basic service in 1986	167	3.02867	0.42752	1.60944	3.98898
LRTBPRICE86	Log of fee for all tiers of basic service in 1986 converted into 1992 dollars	167	2.72638	0.25003	1.97093	3.56267
LOTA86	Log of the number of local broadcast signals offered by the cable franchise on basic service in 1986	183	1.83489	0.62576	0	2.94444
LSAT92	Log of the number of satellite channels offered on all tiers of basic service in 1992	182	2.82348	0.52683	0	3.52636
LTCHAN92	Log of the total number of channels offered for any type of service in 1992	183	3.52184	0.34332	2.48491	4.17439
LTBAS92	Log of the total number of channels offered on all tiers of basic service in 1992	183	3.35971	0.33543	2.30259	4.04305
LRTBPRICE92	Log of fee for all tiers of basic service in 1992	183	2.98516	0.14092	2.30259	3.34109
LOTA	Log of the number of local broadcast signals offered by the cable franchise on basic service in 1992	183	1.90105	0.54015	0	2.83321

Table A-2. *(continued)*

Variable	Definition	Number of observations	Mean	Standard deviation	Minimum	Maximum
REGRM	Franchise was rate regulated in November 1986	176	0.44318	0.49818	0	1.00000
LHH	Log of the number of households in area served by cable system	177	9.24232	1.95201	4.55388	13.21208
LIN	Log of median household income in 1989	183	10.17879	0.35523	9.25300	11.55700
LMSAPOP	Log of the greater of the population of the county or the population of the metropolitan statistical area	183	11.91956	1.89395	8.11013	15.99741
LNONDUP	Log of the number of nonduplicated grade B contour broadcast signals	173	1.83588	0.63774	0	3.17805
POVERTY	Percent of the population below the poverty line	183	13.49231	9.25111	1.61960	57.23020
URBAN	Percent of population residing in an urban area	183	42.90843	41.46823	0	100.00000
OWNER	Percent of housing units that are owner occupied	183	71.98809	15.34404	0.42400	100.00000
CHILD	Percent of households with children	183	36.43661	10.15127	1.52830	88.48680
SINGLE	Percent of households that consist of a single person	183	22.39475	8.30380	0.64240	75.80230
TONGUE	Percent of the population over the age of 5 who speak a language other than English	183	8.00773	13.31138	0	89.93440
EAST	Franchise located in the East	183	0.25137	0.43499	0	1.00000
MW	Franchise located in the Midwest	183	0.23497	0.42514	0	1.00000
SATLANT	Franchise located in the South Atlantic region	183	0.10383	0.30587	0	1.00000
SCENTRAL	Franchise located in the South Central region	183	0.07104	0.25759	0	1.00000
WNOPAC	Franchise located in the Southwest or Mountain states	183	0.18415	0.45225	0	1.00000

Sources: All series are from "FCC Cable TV Rate Survey Database" in MM Docket no. 92-266, March 30, 1994, except for the following; LMSAPOP is based on county-level data from the Census Bureau, and LNONDUP is based on 1992 data from Warren Publishing.

Table A-3. *Parameter Estimates for Reduced-Form Equations for Characteristics of Cable Service, 1986*[a]

Variable	LRTBPRICE86	LTCHAN86	LTBAS	LSAT86	LOTA86
Observations	149	149	149	146	161
Degrees of freedom	132	132	132	129	144
Mean of dependent variable	2.72314	3.21589	3.06008	2.30678	1.86134
Standard error of dependent variable	0.25630	0.42591	0.42952	0.58946	0.61764
Standard error of estimate	0.25599	0.27859	0.28903	0.42772	0.48487
Adjusted R^2	0.00246	0.57213	0.54718	0.47349	0.38372
Constant	3.33147 **	0.98442	0.29990	2.74708	−0.53867
	(2.10137)	(0.57055)	(0.16754)	(1.02998)	(−0.19532)
REGRM	−0.03089	0.02223	0.02754	0.04023	0.00953
	(−0.69872)	(0.46213)	(0.55185)	(0.54217)	(0.11901)
LHH	0.02172	0.07037 ***	0.05709 ***	0.09307 ***	0.03511
	(1.20815)	(3.59646)	(2.81245)	(3.02608)	(1.11013)
LIN	−0.05713	0.00212	0.04312	−0.38246	0.13358
	(−0.36466)	(0.01243)	(0.24376)	(−1.44813)	(0.49248)
LMSAPOP	0.00398	0.05779 ***	0.05580 ***	0.10033 ***	−0.00584
	(0.21238)	(2.83141)	(2.63531)	(3.19313)	(−0.16914)
LNONDUP	−0.07939 *	0.00893	0.03526	−0.00273	0.37770 ***
	(−1.72569)	(0.17845)	(0.67876)	(−0.03518)	(4.37364)
POVERTY	−0.00655	−0.00958 *	−0.00995 *	−0.01609 *	0.00035
	(−1.29848)	(−1.74570)	(−1.74788)	(−1.83682)	(0.03980)

Table A-3. (continued)

Variable	LRTBPRICE86	LTCHAN86	LTBAS	LSAT86	LOTA86
URBAN	0.00064	0.00227 ***	0.00236 ***	0.00328 **	0.00278 **
	(0.83184)	(2.70332)	(2.70072)	(2.52205)	(2.00192)
OWNER	0.00095	0.00275	0.00340	0.00493	0.00451
	(0.44220)	(1.18071)	(1.40560)	(1.36384)	(1.15242)
CHILD	-0.00068	0.00816	0.01037 **	0.01048	-0.00041
	(-0.14910)	(1.64038)	(2.00849)	(1.36560)	(-0.04933)
SINGLE	-0.00104	0.01124 *	0.01451 **	0.01294	0.00383
	(-0.17975)	(1.77932)	(2.21414)	(1.32840)	(0.36390)
TONGUE	-0.00273	0.00297	0.00241	0.00754 **	-0.00521
	(-1.32283)	(1.31791)	(1.03454)	(2.15627)	(-1.36177)
EAST	-0.12238	0.06960	0.09228	0.27022 *	-0.41008 ***
	(-1.45673)	(0.76125)	(0.97284)	(1.89150)	(-2.66614)
MW	-0.08378	0.10035	0.10412	0.33338 **	-0.36479 **
	(-1.01844)	(1.12085)	(1.12091)	(2.41387)	(-2.42419)
SATLANT	0.00193	0.05757	0.08403	0.41367 **	-0.41920
	(0.01900)	(0.52146)	(0.73355)	(2.43231)	(-2.22453)
SCENTRAL	0.00754	-0.05620	-0.00820	0.05902	-0.34238
	(0.06417)	(-0.43976)	(-0.06187)	(0.29173)	(-1.59353)
WNOPAC	-0.02887	0.08969	0.09704	0.42723 ***	-0.56957 ***
	(-0.34157)	(0.97500)	(1.01676)	(3.01294)	(-3.68819)

Sources: See table A-2.

a. t-statistics in parentheses.

* Significantly different from zero at 10 percent confidence interval.

** Significantly different from zero at 5 percent confidence interval.

*** Significantly different from zero at 1 percent confidence interval.

Table A-4. *Parameters from the Two-Stage Least-Squares Estimation of the Characteristics of Cable Service in 1992, Holding 1986 Characteristics Constant*[a]

Variable	LRTBPRICE92	LTCHAN92	LTBAS92	LSAT92	LOTA92
Observations	149	149	149	145	161
Degrees of freedom	142	142	142	138	154
Mean of dependent variable	2.99096	3.55924	3.39462	2.88986	1.92075
Standard error of dependent variable	0.14105	0.33845	0.33778	0.50004	0.53776
Standard error of estimate	0.13000	0.17149	0.18552	0.33720	0.31514
Adjusted R^2	0.15049	0.74326	0.69833	0.54524	0.65659
Constant	2.26664 ***	1.23737 ***	1.16363 ***	1.17938 ***	−0.07425
	(4.60750)	(5.58265)	(5.12271)	(5.00368)	(−0.32557)
REGRM	0.04639 **	0.03992	0.04617	0.09805 *	0.03648
	(2.04754)	(1.39326)	(1.48996)	(1.73078)	(0.72021)
LHH	0.01666 **	0.06923 ***	0.06776 ***	0.07822 ***	0.02932
	(2.05416)	(4.28931)	(4.22260)	(3.05863)	(1.63163)
LMSAPOP	−0.00108	−0.01640	−0.01440	−0.05330 **	0.04234 **
	(−0.12150)	(−1.09404)	(−0.90484)	(−1.99314)	(2.03320)

Table A-4. (continued)

Variable	LRTBPRICE92	LTCHAN92	LTBAS92	LSAT92	LOTA92
LNONDUP	0.01742	0.01912	0.00387	0.05274	0.05199
	(0.69378)	(0.65141)	(0.12250)	(0.89292)	(0.58091)
POVERTY	−0.00051	0.00330 *	0.00361 *	0.00411	0.00497
	(−0.32594)	(1.73989)	(1.71351)	(1.13961)	(1.57780)
LRTBPRICE86	0.19603	...	...	...	0.55475 ***
	(1.11239)				(3.68753)
LTCHAN86	...	0.54986 ***	...	...	...
		(4.34301)			
LTBAS86	...	...	0.55183 ***	...	...
			(4.14546)		
LSAT86	...	...	...	0.61285 ***	...
				(4.87637)	
LOTA86	...	...	...	...	0.55475 ***
					(3.68753)

Sources: See table A-2. Instruments: Constant, REGRM, LHH, LIN, LMSAPOP, LNONDUP, POVERTY, URBAN, OWNER, CHILD, SINGLE, TONGUE, EAST, MW, SATLANT, SCENTRAL, WNOPAC.
a. t-statistics in parentheses.
* Significantly different from zero at 10 percent confidence interval.
** Significantly different from zero at 5 percent confidence interval.
*** Significantly different from zero at 1 percent confidence interval.

Estimation of Demand for Cable Television from Household Data

$\mathbf{A}$PPENDIX A discussed some of the limitations in the current economics literature on the demand for cable television services. These limitations are partly caused by the use of cable system franchise-level data rather than more disaggregated data. This appendix introduces models of household-level demand for cable services that avoid some of the problems of models based on more aggregated data.

Choice Set

Cable television services are part of a large and expanding array of entertainment and information choices available to U.S. households.[1] Some of these choices, such as movie theaters, lead to entertainment away from home; others, such as cable television, lead to entertainment at home. Not all households face the same entertainment choice set, and partly as a consequence, not all households are equally likely to subscribe to cable television. To examine the likelihood that a household will subscribe to cable television, we partitioned the entertainment choice set into two subsets: the subset of cable television options conditional on a household's having immediate access to cable television; and the complement of this subset, all entertainment options other than cable television. Access to cable is a necessary prerequisite for a household to face the choices that this appendix explores. The breadth of the second subset of entertainment options determines the number of possible substitutes for cable television. The like-

---

1. For most practical purposes, demand for cable television is measured by households rather than individuals. Although cable bills are addressed to one individual within a household, no additional fees are levied based directly on the number of household members. Cable fees may increase with demand for some services that are related to the number of household members, such as the number of additional outlets and the number of remote control devices.

lihood of subscribing to cable may reasonably diminish with the diversity of other entertainment options and with decreasing relative prices of at least some of those options.

Unit of Analysis

We analyzed household demand for cable services based on two surveys: one from early 1992 and one from spring 1993. We obtained the household data from Allison Fisher, a consumer survey firm. It supplied the responses to a questionnaire on demographic and consumption patterns from a sample of 750 households in winter 1992; of these, 664 responded. The questionnaire included information on whether the household subscribed to cable television and whether it subscribed to premium channels.

With data from Warren Publishing we constructed a data set of the service characteristics of the cable systems that served the households in both the 1992 and 1993 surveys.[2] For each cable system, we obtained information on channel lineups, prices, and other system characteristics for 1992 and—if the system was operational then—for 1983–84.[3] Some of the 664 households responding to the 1992 survey did not provide complete information, and others were not passed by cable; we excluded both from our final data set.[4] We also excluded households for which we were not able to find current information on cable characteristics from Warren Publishing.[5] Ultimately, we had complete information on all of the variables in our multinomial logit model for 441 households from the 1992 survey.

We supplemented the winter 1992 questionnaire with one in May and June 1993 that requested cable-specific information from the same sample of 750 households. We used this data set to examine household choice of specific premium channels. From this second questionnaire, 488 households responded, of which we have complete information for 281.

---

2. Warren Publishing, *Television and Cable Factbook* (Washington, 1992, 1993).

3. Information from this earlier period is used for the measurement of changes in consumer welfare in chapter 3 for about a ten-year period.

4. Although information on cable availability was not included in the 1992 survey, this information was included in the 1993 survey. There was a substantial overlap in households between the 1992 and 1993 surveys, and we assumed that households not passed by cable in 1993 were also not passed by cable in 1992.

5. We excluded cable systems whose most recent reported information was before January 1991.

Access to Cable Television

The first prerequisite for cable subscription is access to a cable system. Access has expanded steadily throughout the past two decades. By 1993 only 3 percent of American households were not passed by cable and, short of moving, these households could not obtain video services from a cable operator at any price. For these households decisions about cable subscription are not relevant. For our 1993 sample of 479 households responding to the question, 58, or about 12 percent, reported not being passed by cable. Consequently, a greater proportion of households in our survey than in the nation at large does not have cable access.[6]

The second prerequisite for cable subscription is television ownership. The rate of television ownership increased steadily from 1945 through 1970, and has remained relatively constant at nearly 99 percent since then.[7] In a society in which television ownership is nearly universal, a decision not to own a television set may reflect low income or disinterest or even dissatisfaction with the programming available or the price of the programming. For our 1993 sample of 488 households responding to the question, only 1, or less than 0.3 percent, did not own a television. Thus our sample reflects television ownership nationwide. For households without televisions, we assumed that decisions about cable subscription were not immediately relevant.[8]

Factors Influencing Household Demand

Demand for cable television depends on many factors, but they can be placed into three broad categories: geographic characteristics of the community in which the household is located, cable system characteristics, and household characteristics.

6. Alternatively, some of these households may have incorrectly responded that they were not passed by cable.

7. See Arbitron and Nielsen data as reported in Warren Publishing, *Television and Cable Factbook* (Washington, 1945–70).

8. If cable prices were to decrease or cable quality to improve, some portion of these nontelevision households might purchase a television and subscribe. We are not in a position to estimate the effect of cable prices or quality on television ownership. Television ownership patterns by household in the United States have been remarkably constant over the past twenty-five years.

Geographic Characteristics

Geography may exert a strong influence on whether a household sub-scribes to cable and whether it subscribes to premium channels. For example, households in communities with a wide array of alternative and easily accessible forms of entertainment may be less likely to subscribe to cable than those in smaller, more confining communities. We expected that communities with larger populations have a greater diversity of entertainment choices. We examined the effect on household cable demand of the following measures of community size: county population, Census Bureau measures of county characteristics, and the size of the Department of Commerce metropolitan statistical area. Of these variables, we found that residence outside an MSA, that is, in a rural area, was the best predictor of choosing to subscribe.

Communities with large numbers of over-the-air broadcast signals might reasonably be expected to have less cable penetration than communities with few signals.[9] Our measure of the availability of broadcast signals is the number of nonduplicated broadcast stations within whose grade B contours a household is located.[10]

Most households have access to video services other than cable, such as satellite subscription or direct broadcast satellite, and some communities have access to local wireless competitors such as MMDS. The availability, price, and quality of these services will affect the demand for cable television.[11] Although they were not widely subscribed in 1992, these services are increasingly common and are likely to have more subscribers in the future. Unfortunately, because there are no reasonably comprehensive

9. This effect of over-the-air broadcast signals on the price and demand for cable television has been documented in the research of Robert W. Crandall, "Elasticity of Demand for Cable Service and the Effect of Broadcast Signals on Cable Prices," appended to TCI Comments in MM Docket no. 90-4, April 16, 1990; James N. Dertouzos and Steven S. Wildman, "Competitive Effects of Broadcast Signals on Cable," paper prepared for the National Cable Television Association, March 1, 1990; and Mark M. Bykowsky and Tim Sloan, "Competitive Effects of Broadcast Signals on the Price of Basic Service," Office of Policy Analysis and Development staff paper, National Telecommunications and Information Administration, April 6, 1990.

10. Warren Publishing, *Cable & Station Coverage Atlas* (Washington, 1994). Specifically, we defined the number of nonduplicated signals as the sum of the number of nonduplicated commercial networks, the number of independent commercial stations, and a value of one for the presence of at least one public or educational station.

11. John W. Mayo and Yasuji Otsuka, "Demand, Pricing, and Regulation: Evidence from the Cable TV Industry," *RAND Journal of Economics,* vol. 22 (Autumn 1991), pp. 396–410, found a significant effect of these alternatives on the demand for cable television.

data on the local differences in availability, price, and quality of the services, we did not control for them.

Finally, holding other measurable factors constant, households in different regions may be more or less inclined to subscribe to cable. These regional differences may reflect climate or the cost of living. We examined broad regional differences in demand equations and found no systematic differences.

System Characteristics

Cable system subscriptions may increase with the age of the system, an observation made in the early 1970s by Comanor and Mitchell; Park; and Noll, Peck, and McGowan.[12] The same relationship has been found in subsequent research.[13] Prolonged exposure to information about cable services and promotional offerings from operators may increase the likelihood of a household's subscribing to cable services. We used the number of years between the date of initial service and February 1, 1992, as the measure of system age.

The likelihood of cable subscription is also strongly influenced by the quality of the service, which of course varies from system to system. Measures of quality are not easily defined. We used the number of satellite-based basic cable networks as one of our primary measures.[14] We expected that increases in the number of cable channels might be associated with improved quality. In particular, we expected that more basic satellite-

---

12. William S. Comanor and Bridger M. Mitchell, "Cable Television and the Impact of Regulation," *Bell Journal of Economics and Management Science,* vol. 2 (Spring 1971), pp. 154–212; Rolla Edward Park, "Prospects for Cable in the 100 Largest Television Markets," *Bell Journal of Economics and Management Science,* vol. 3 (Spring 1972), pp. 130–50; and Roger G. Noll, Merton J. Peck, and John J. McGowan, *Economic Aspects of Television Regulation* (Brookings, 1973).

13. See Mayo and Otsuka, 'Demand, Pricing, and Regulation"; and Robert N. Rubinovitz, "Market Power and Price Increases for Basic Cable Service Since Deregulation, *RAND Journal of Economics,* vol. 24 (Spring 1993), pp. 1–18.

14. In additon, we examined the effect of the number of channels within specific categories of programming such as sports or movies. We found few measurable effects of the number of channels within these categories. We also examined the number of other types of channels such as premium channels; public, educational, and governmental channels; and unused capacity. We found that the number of these channels has much less influence on the basic subscription decision than does either the number of broadcast networks or the number of basic satellite-based networks.

based networks offered on a cable system would encourage greater subscription to basic services.[15]

Our second measure of quality was the number of broadcast stations that a cable system carried and received off the air or by microwave.[16] Broadcast signals are sources of information and entertainment of local interest. Moreover, they are the primary distribution source for the major broadcast networks. Although in 1992 cable systems did not pay for local broadcast signals, cable operators paid copyright royalties for distant signals, generally those originating more than thirty-five miles away.[17] Consequently, distant broadcast signals are required to pass a threshold of higher cost—and presumably a higher minimum value to subscribers—than local broadcast signals.[18]

Aside from cable networks and broadcast signals, the only channels available to the basic subscriber are those required by the local franchising authority—nonbroadcast public, educational, and governmental channels.[19] We found little effect on basic cable subscriptions from the number of these channels. The channels are often offered by systems not in response to market demand but rather as a condition of franchise service.

Perhaps the most important system characteristic influencing basic subscription is the price of basic services, which varies considerably among communities. The higher the price, holding other factors constant, the less likely a household is to subscribe. The price of premium services may not have as pronounced an effect on subscription. Nonetheless, we expected that the price of basic service influenced a household's willingness to subscribe to both basic and premium services. In addition, we included the price of premium service and the number of premium services as explanatory variables in the premium-service equation.

15. Of course, not all cable networks are identical. Consequently, we did not expect that any combination of n basic cable networks is always preferred by a household to any other combination of $n - 1$ basic networks.

16. These broadcast signals may have included local and some distant stations. A cable headend has sophisticated equipment that may enable the operator to receive distant signals that a household cannot ordinarily receive. Superstations, such as WTBS and WGN, are broadcast in their city of origin and distributed nationally via satellite. We counted satellite-distributed superstations as cable networks.

17. The formula for copyright royalties on distant broadcast signals is complex and depends on the size of the television market and the number of distant broadcast signals carried. We have treated distant broadcast signals that are distributed by satellites, such as superstations, as satellite-based networks.

18. This is not to say that all distant broadcast signals are more valuable than local broadcast signals; rather, the threshold for inclusion of distant signals is higher than the threshold for local signals.

19. All broadcast channels, both commercial and public, are counted as a measure of the quality of service.

Household Characteristics

Differences in household characteristics may lead to significant differences in the likelihood of subscribing to cable. We expected that both basic and premium cable television subscriptions are normal goods; as a household's income rises, it is more likely to subscribe to cable. The effect of income on the likelihood of subscription may differ among premium cable services.

The likelihood of cable subscription may also depend on such demographic characteristics as age and family size. Families with young children or with elderly members may subscribe more frequently. Different premium channels may be attractive to households with certain demographic characteristics. Another important characteristic is length of residency; short-time residents may be transients (for example, college students) who may not believe that their length of stay warrants an investment in the installation cost of basic cable. At the other extreme, long-time residents may be slower to adopt new technologies than newer residents; new homeowners may be more inclined to subscribe.

Household equipment, including musical instruments, stereo equipment, video games, and video cassette recorders, may also influence the choice of entertainment options. The effect of owning a VCR or other equipment on household cable subscription decisions is not obvious a priori. On the one hand, because VCR usage may substitute for cable viewing, VCR ownership might reduce the likelihood of cable subscription. On the other hand, a VCR could complement cable television by allowing the recording of programming for later or repeated viewing and increase the likelihood of cable subscription. Alternatively, VCR ownership may simply signal intense interest in video services. Thus there are many reasons cable subscription patterns of VCR owners differ from those of nonowners.

We examined the effect on cable demand of other household characteristics such as the education of the head of household, the gender of the head of household, and the presence of children. None was a useful predictor of cable demand in the multinomial logit model.

A Multinomial Logit Model for Household Purchase of Cable Services

The smallest unit of observation for demand for cable television services is the household. Cable subscriptions apply to households rather than individuals.[20] Consider the following general representation of household i's indirect utility V^{ilt}, $i = 1, \ldots, T$, based on a discrete choice of cable service options at time t at location l:

(B.1) $$V^{ilt} = V(\mathbf{p}^{slt}, p^{1lt}, p^{2lt}, \mathbf{q}^{slt}, \mathbf{q}^{1lt}, \mathbf{q}^{2lt}, \mathbf{Z}^{it}, \mathbf{Z}^{lt}, Y^{it}, \mathbf{P}^{lt}, \mathbf{\eta}^{it}, \mathbf{\eta}^{lt}),$$

where $\mathbf{p}^{slt}$ is a vector of the unobserved prices of the substitutes for cable services at location l at time t;[21] p^{1lt} is the price for basic cable services at location l at time t;[22] p^{2lt} is the combined price for basic and premium cable services at location l at time t;[23] $\mathbf{q}^{slt}$ is a vector of the quality of substitute services;[24] $\mathbf{q}^{1lt}$ is a vector of the quality of basic cable services at location l at time t;[25] $\mathbf{q}^{2lt}$ is a vector of the quality of the combined basic and premium

20. Cable television is a household rather than an individual expenditure. Utility functions and demand functions can be interpreted with household-level data. Our treatment of demand for cable television would have a distinct but analogous derivation through profit functions for hotels, bars, and other commercial establishments that subscribe to cable television.

21. Substitute services are potentially other entertainment and information services. These include the rental of an antenna for better reception of broadcast signals, video cassette rentals, motion picture theaters, athletic events, newspapers, books, and other entertainment and information services. We have no local measures of these prices. Various demographic and regional variables are likely to serve as proxies for these substitute prices.

22. Using data from Warren Publishing, we observe the fees for tiers of basic service. In 1992 when our first survey was conducted, cable operators often had ordered tiers of service with buy-through requirements such that subscription to one tier of service required subscription to all lower tiers of service. For systems with only one tier of basic service, we set the price for basic service equal to the fee for that tier. For systems with more than one tier of basic service, we use the price of the tier with the greatest number of subscribers, which in practically every system is the highest tier of service. We do not observe the prices for all equipment and services associated with basic subscription such as installation fees and rental fees for additional outlets or remote controls. The prices of these additional services and equipment are not necessarily associated with the channel lineup.

23. The combined price is the relevant price faced by households because cable systems do not allow purchase of premium channels without purchase of basic service as well. Most systems offer more than one premium service, and, for our 1992 sample, we do not observe household selection patterns. We use the price of the widely available HBO network as a proxy for the price of premium channels.

24. These quality attributes include the number of broadcast signals that can be received locally and other local characteristics such as the variety and quality of local entertainment and information. Of these, we have a direct measurement only of local broadcast signals. We examined several variables to measure local broadcast signals including the number of nonduplicated signals, the number of independent stations, and several dichotomous variables indicating whether a certain minimum number of broadcast signals was available. Of these variables, the number of nonduplicated signals was the best predictor of demand. We also include a constant term in $\mathbf{q}^{slt}$.

25. The basic cable quality vector that we use includes the number of satellite-based networks and the number of broadcast signals received by the cable operator off the air or by microwave.

services;[26] Z^{it} is a vector of the observable household-specific characteristics of household i at time t;[27] Z^{lt} is a vector of the observable location-specific characteristics of location l at time t;[28] Y^{it} is household income of household i at time t; P^{lt} is a vector of all other prices faced by the household at location l at time t;[29] η^{it} is a vector of unobservable household-specific characteristics of household i at time t; and η^{lt} is a vector of unobservable location-specific characteristics of location l at time t.

Each household that owns a television set and is passed by a cable system faces three distinct, mutually exclusive choices with respect to cable televisions services: (0) do not subscribe to cable services; (1) subscribe to basic cable only; or (2) subscribe to basic plus premium cable services.[30] We further assumed that there is an unobserved latent variable, v_j^*, associated with each choice, j equals 0,1,2, corresponding to the indirect utility derived from subscription to no cable services, basic cable services, and basic plus at least one premium cable service, that may be expressed as[31]

26. Although different cable systems have different premium channel offerings, we do not attempt to adjust for differences in premium channel quality because we do not observe the actual premium channel selection by the household. We measure the quality of premium service by the number of available premium channels, and again we measure the quality of basic service by the number of satellite-based networks and the number of broadcast signals received by the cable operator off the air or by microwave.

27. These characteristics include the number of persons in the household, the age of the head of household, the duration of residency, and VCR ownership.

28. These characteristics include the population of the county in which the household resides, the extent of ruralness and urbanness of the county, average per capita income in the county, and the region of the country. Among these variables, we found that a dichotomous variable indicating whether a household is inside or outside of an MSA was the best predictor of demand.

29. These are prices of goods and services that are not directly substitutable with cable services. For comparisons over time, we use the consumer price index for this price vector. We use this price vector as the numeraire and set it to one in each time period.

30. In January 1992 roughly 99 percent of all households in the continental United States had a television set. See Warren Publishing, *Television & Cable Factbook* (1992), p. G-20. The percentage of U.S. households with television sets did not change appreciably between 1983 and 1992. Compare Warren Publishing, *Television & Cable Factbook* (1984), p. 40. Our analysis examines for television households the choice between different sources of television programming, and not whether different prices and quality of cable programming have induced or discouraged television ownership. Consequently, we have excluded from our sample those households that do not use a television.

In 1992, of the 93.05 million television households in the continental United States, 90.6 million were passed by a cable system. Consequently, 2.45 million households did not have access to cable. Paul Kagan Associates, *Kagan Media Index,* March 30, 1993.

31. The latent variables may vary with intensity of use and other unobserved factors related to usage.

(B.2a) $v_0^{*ilt} = v_0^*(\mathbf{p}^{st}, \mathbf{q}^{slt}, \mathbf{Z}^{it}, \mathbf{Z}^{lt}, Y^{it}, \mathbf{P}^{lt}, \boldsymbol{\eta}^{it}, \boldsymbol{\eta}^{lt}),$

(B.2b) $v_1^{*ilt} = v_1^*(p^{1t}, \mathbf{q}^{1lt}, \mathbf{Z}^{it}, \mathbf{Z}^{lt}, Y^{it}, \mathbf{P}^{lt}, \boldsymbol{\eta}^{it}, \boldsymbol{\eta}^{lt}),$

(B.2c) $v_2^{*ilt} = v_2^*(p^{2t}, \mathbf{q}^{2lt}, \mathbf{Z}^{it}, \mathbf{Z}^{lt}, Y^{it}, \mathbf{P}^{lt}, \boldsymbol{\eta}^{it}, \boldsymbol{\eta}^{lt}).$

Let $V^{*ilt} = \text{Max}\ (v_0^{*ilt}, v_1^{*ilt}, v_2^{*ilt})$. Although we do not observe the latent variables, v_j^{*ilt}, we do observe the choices $j = 0, 1, 2$. We denote these choice variables as

(B.3) $v_j^{ilt} = 1$ if $v_j^{*ilt} = V^{*ilt}$

           $= 0$ otherwise.

We assume that the indirect utility function, in addition to satisfying the usual properties of indirect utility functions,[32] also satisfies random utility maximization and a variant of Roy's Identity for prices associated with discrete choices:[33]

(B.4) $- \partial V^{*ilt}/\partial p^{jlt}\ [\partial V^{*ilt}/\partial Y^{it}]^{-1} = 1$ if $v_j^{*ilt} = V^{*ilt}$

           $= 0$ otherwise.

We partition the unconditional indirect utility function in equation B.1 into three components:

(B.5) $V^{ilt} = W(\mathbf{p}^{slt}, p^{1lt}, p^{2lt}, \mathbf{q}^{slt}, \mathbf{q}^{1lt}, \mathbf{q}^{2lt}, \mathbf{Z}^{it}, \mathbf{Z}^{lt}, Y^i)$

           $+ H^i(Y^{it}) + E(\mathbf{P}^{lt}, \boldsymbol{\eta}^{it}, \boldsymbol{\eta}^{lt}),$

where W is a conditional indirect utility function that applies for all households for discrete choices involving cable television;[34] H^i is a household-

---

32. An indirect utility function v is a function of prices p, income y, and potentially other factors z, and is the solution to the maximization problem

$\mathbf{v}(\mathbf{p}, y, z) = \max[u(\mathbf{x}, z) : \mathbf{p} \cdot \mathbf{x} \leq y]$

for a utility function $u(x, z)$. The properties of the indirect utility function are described in W. E. Diewert, "Applications of Duality Theory," in Michael D. Intriligator and David A. Kendrick, eds., *Frontiers of Quantitative Economics*, vol. 2 (Amsterdam: North Holland, 1969). More specifically, an indirect utility function is (1) nonincreasing in prices; (2) quasiconvex in prices; (3) increasing in income; and (4) homogeneous of degree zero in prices and income. To these properties, we add that the indirect utility function is nondecreasing in quality attributes q. See also Hal R. Varian, *Microeconomic Analysis* (Norton, 1978), pp. 89–90; and Daniel McFadden, "Econometric Models of Probabilistic Choice," in Charles F. Manski and Daniel McFadden, eds., *Structural Analysis of Discrete Data with Econometric Applications* (MIT Press, 1981), pp. 202–08.

33. See McFadden, "Econometric Models of Probabilistic Choice," pp. 202–08.

34. See Kenneth A. Small and Harvey S. Rosen, "Applied Welfare Economics with Discrete Choice Models," *Econometrica*, vol. 49 (January 1981), p. 123, on the partition of the indirect utility function into separable additive components and conditional indirect utility functions.

specific component of the utility function; and E is a function of the remaining variables. In practice, we observe choices v_j, but we do not observe the variables $(\mathbf{P}^{lt}, \mathbf{\eta}^{it}, \mathbf{\eta}^{lt})$. We restate equation B.5 as

$$(\text{B.6}) \quad V^{ilt} = W(\mathbf{p}^{slt}, p^{1lt}, p^{2lt}, \mathbf{q}^{slt}, \mathbf{q}^{1lt}, \mathbf{q}^{2lt}, \mathbf{Z}^{it}, \mathbf{Z}^{lt}, Y^{it}) + H^i(Y^{it}) + \epsilon^{ilt},$$

where ϵ^{ilt} is a random variable reflecting in part the values of $(\mathbf{P}^{lt}, \mathbf{\eta}^{it}, \mathbf{\eta}^{lt})$ but independent of the arguments of W.

From equations (B.2a) through (B.2c), we designate the unobserved latent variables v_j^* associated with each choice, $j = 0,1,2$ as

$$(\text{B.7}) \qquad v_j^{*ilt} = W_j^*(p^{jlt}, \mathbf{q}^{jlt}, \mathbf{Z}^{it}, \mathbf{Z}^{lt}, Y^{it}) + H^i(Y^{it}) + \epsilon_j^{*ilt}.$$

Let $W^{*ilt} = \text{Max}\,(W_0^* + \epsilon_0^{*ilt}, W_1^* + \epsilon_1^{*ilt}, W_2^* + \epsilon_2^{*ilt})$. Although we do not observe the latent variables v_j^{*ilt}, we do observe the choices $j = 0,1,2$. Notice that the value of $H^i(Y^{it})$ is the same for all j. Define

$$h_j^{*ilt} = v_i^{*ilt} - H^i(Y^{it}) = W_j^* + \epsilon_j^{*ilt}.$$

Then, $W^{*ilt} = \text{Max}\,(h_j^{*ilt}; j = 0,1,2)$, and $W^{*ilt} = V^{*ilt} - H^i(Y^{it})$. Consequently, from equation (B.3),

$$(\text{B.8}) \qquad v_j^{ilt} = 1 \text{ if } v_j^{*ilt} = V^{*ilt}, \text{ or equivalently, if } h_j^{*ilt} = W^*$$
$$= 0 \text{ otherwise.}$$

Set $\lambda = [\partial V^{*ilt}/\partial Y^{it}] = [\partial W^*/\partial Y^{it} + \partial H^{*i}/\partial Y^{it}]$, the marginal indirect utility of income. Equation (B.4) may be restated as

$$(\text{B.9}) \, \partial V^{*ilt}/\partial p^{jlt}\,\lambda^{-1} = -\partial W^*/\partial p^{jlt}\,[\partial W^*/\partial Y^{it} + \partial H^{*i}/\partial Y^{it}]^{-1}$$
$$= -\partial W^*/\partial p^{jlt}\,\lambda^{-1}$$
$$= 1 \text{ if } v_j^{*ilt} = V^{*ilt} \text{ or equivalently, if } h_j^{*ilt} = W$$
$$= 0 \text{ otherwise.}$$

We further assume that the cumulative distribution function of ϵ_j^{*ilt} can be expressed as having a Weibull distribution:

$$(\text{B.10}) \qquad\qquad F(\epsilon_j^{*ilt} < \epsilon) = \exp(-e^{-\epsilon})$$

and with probability density function

$$(\text{B.11}) \qquad\qquad f(\epsilon_j^{*ilt}) = \exp[-\epsilon_j^{*ilt} - \exp(-\epsilon_j^{*ilt})].$$

Then,

(B.12) $\text{Prob}(v_j^{ilt} = 1; j = 0,1,2) = \exp(W_j^*) \cdot [\exp(W_0^*)$

$$+ \exp(W_1^*) + \exp(W_2^*)]^{-1}.[35]$$

We express $W_j^* (p^{ilt}, q^{ilt}, Z^{it}, Z^{lt}, Y^{it})$ as a linear combination:

(B.13) $\qquad W_j^* = [p^{ilt}]\mathbf{b} + [q^{ilt}]\mathbf{g}_j + [Z^{it}, Z^{lt}, Y^{it}]\mathbf{d}_j$

$\qquad$ or $h_j^{*ilt} = [\mathbf{p}^{ilt}]\mathbf{b} + [\mathbf{q}^{ilt}]\mathbf{g}_j + [Z^{it}, Z^{lt}, Y^{it}]\mathbf{d}_j + e_j^{*ilt},$

where $[q^{ilt}]$ is a vector of quality attributes for each choice j; $\mathbf{g}_j$ is a corresponding vector of parameters for each option j;[36] $[Z^{it}, Z^{lt}, Y^{it}]$ is a $T \times K$ matrix of household- and location-specific observations, $i = 1, \ldots, T$; and $\mathbf{d}_j$ is a $K \times 1$ vector of parameters that varies for each option j.

Combining equations (B.12) and (B.13), we have

(B.14) $\qquad \text{Prob}(v_j^{ilt} = 1; j = 0,1,2)$

$$= (\exp([p^{ilt}]\mathbf{b} + [q^{ilt}]\mathbf{g}_j + [Z^{it}, Z^{lt}, Y^{it}]\mathbf{d}_j)) *$$

$$\left[\sum_{k=0}^{2} \exp([p^{klt}]\mathbf{b} + [q^{klt}]\mathbf{g}_k + [Z^{it}, Z^{lt}, Y^{it}]\mathbf{d}_k) \right]^{-1}$$

Equation (B.14) requires some normalization for $\mathbf{g}_j$ and $\mathbf{d}_j$ to be identified.[37] Because the costs of basic and premium services are essentially incremental costs beyond no cable services, we can scale the cost of no cable service to zero. Consequently, we set W_0^* to zero by setting $\mathbf{g}_0 = 0$, $\mathbf{d}_0 = 0$, and $p^{0lt} = 0$. Then

---

35. See Daniel McFadden, "Conditional Logit Analysis of Qualitative Choice Behavior," in Paul Zarembka, ed., *Frontiers in Econometrics* (Academic Press, 1974), pp. 105–42; G. S. Maddala, *Limited Dependent and Qualitative Variables in Econometrics* (Cambridge University Press, 1986), pp. 59–61; and William H. Greene, *Econometric Analysis* (Macmillan, 1993), pp. 664–65.

36. In a conditional multinomial logit specification, the coefficients of q^{ilt} would be constant across all options j. See Maddala, *Limited Dependent and Qualitative Variables in Econometrics,* p. 61; and Greene, *Econometric Analysis,* pp. 665–69. The characteristics of cable television, however, are such that there is no single measure of quality that varies across the different cable choices. The number of satellite-delivered basic networks and the number of off-the-air signals are the same for basic and premium subscribers. Only the number of premium channels is unique to one tier, the premium tier. Consequently, we allow the coefficients on the quality measures to vary across the choices. We also test the restriction of holding these coefficients constant across the cable choices.

37. See Greene, *Econometric Analysis,* p. 666.

(B.15) $\text{Prob}(v_\phi{}^{ilt} = 1)$

$$= \left[1 + \sum_{k=1}^{2} (\exp([p^{klt}]\mathbf{b} + [\mathbf{q}^{klt}]\mathbf{g}_k + [Z^{it}, Z^{lt}, Y^{it}]\mathbf{d}_k)) \right]^{-1}$$

and $\text{Prob}(v_j{}^{ilt} = 1; j = 1,2)$

$$= [\exp([p^{jlt}]\mathbf{b} + [\mathbf{q}^{jlt}]\mathbf{g}_j + [Z^{it}, Z^{lt}, Y^{it}]\mathbf{d}_j)] *$$

$$\left[1 + \sum_{k=1}^{2} \exp([p^{klt}]\mathbf{b} + [\mathbf{q}^{klt}]\mathbf{g}_k + [Z^{it}, Z^{lt}, Y^{it}]\mathbf{d}_k) \right]^{-1}.$$

Sample Statistics

We estimate the multinomial logit model (B.15) based on the following variables:

$p^{1/92}$: (*PRICE*) = the price for basic cable services at location *l* in early 1992;

$p^{2/92}$: (*PREMP*) = the combined price for basic and premium cable services at location *l* in early 1992;

$\mathbf{q}^{1/92}$: quality of basic cable service defined by the following:[38]
CONSTANT = 1;
BASAT = number of channels of programming on basic tiers delivered by satellite in early 1992;[39]
OFFAIR = number of channels of programming on basic tiers received by the headend either off the air or by microwave in early 1992;

$\mathbf{q}^{2/92}$: quality of basic plus premium cable service defined by the following:
CONSTANT = 1;
BASAT = number of satellite channels on basic tiers in early 1992;
OFFAIR = number of channels of programming on basic tiers received by the headend either off the air or by microwave in early 1992;
PREM = number of available premium channels in early 1992;

Z^{i92}: household attributes in early 1992 defined by the following dummy variables:[40]

38. All data for price and quality of service are from Warren Publishing.
39. Both cable-only networks and distant broadcast super stations are delivered by satellite.
40. All measures are based on data from Allison Fisher. These variables have a value of unity if the characteristic applies to the household and a value of zero otherwise.

AGE65 = head of household is older than sixty-four;
TIME5 = household at current address for more than five years;
FSIZE1 = household has one member;
VCR = VCR ownership;

Y^{i92}: (Y) = household monthly income in early 1992;[41]
Z^{l92}: (Z) = locational attributes in early 1992 defined by the following:
GRADEB = number of broadcast signals within a Grade B contour;
RURA = household located outside of metropolitan statistical area;[42]
LSYSAGE = log of the age of the cable system.[43]

The 1983 characteristics are

$p^{1/83}$: (*PRICE8392*) = the price for basic cable services at location *l* in 1983 indexed in 1992 dollars;[44]
p^{2lt}: (*PREMP8392*) = the combined price for basic and premium cable services at location *l* in 1983 indexed in 1992 dollars;
$q^{k/83}$: quality of cable service defined by the following:[45]

Basic, $k = 1$:

CONSTANT = 1;
BASAT83 = number of channels of programming on basic tiers delivered by satellite in 1983–84;[46]
OFFAIR83 = number of channels of programming on basic tiers received by headend either off the air or by microwave in 1983–84.

Basic plus premium, $k = 2$:

CONSTANT = 1;
OFFAIR83 = number of channels of programming on basic tiers received by headend either off the air or by microwave in 1983–84;

---

41. For our household samples from Allison Fisher, our measure of household income was based on self-reported income, presumably pretax, at intervals of approximately $5,000 rather than actual dollar amounts. In our data set, we cannot distinguish the income between households with similar but different incomes, nor can we detect any misrepresentations in the reporting of income.
42. Based on information from Allison Fisher.
43. Based on data from Warren Publishing.
44. All price data are from Warren Publishing.
45. All data for quality of service are from Warren Publishing.
46. Both cable-only networks and distant broadcast super stations are delivered by satellite.

Table B-1. *Sample Statistics for Variables in Multinomial Logit Model, 1992 Sample*

Variable	Number of observations	Mean	Standard deviation	Minimum	Maximum
1992 characteristics					
PRICE	441	19.59	3.58	7.00	35.90
BASAT	441	23.16	5.97	1.00	38.00
NONDUP	441	6.17	2.36	0.00	15.00
OFFAIR	441	8.79	3.24	0.00	18.00
RURA	441	0.19	0.39	0.00	1.00
SYSAGE	441	19.07	8.05	1.94	41.01
Y	441	3,073.79	2,492.84	416.00	14,583.00
AGE65	441	0.21	0.41	0.00	1.00
TIMES	441	0.56	0.50	0.00	1.00
FSIZE1	441	0.25	0.43	0.00	1.00
PREM	441	5.29	1.61	0.00	11.00
PREMP	441	30.10	3.94	16.70	45.85
VCR	441	0.69	0.46	0.00	1.00
Choice = no cable	441	0.32	0.47	0.00	1.00
Choice = basic only	441	0.39	0.49	0.00	1.00
Choice = basic and premium	441	0.29	0.45	0.00	1.00
1983–84 characteristics					
PRICE8392	278	14.07	3.35	6.54	34.12
BASAT83	278	10.04	6.44	0.00	25.00
PREM83	278	2.88	1.76	1.00	8.00
PREMP8392	278	29.23	4.97	17.32	59.26
OFFAIR83	278	9.59	3.30	3.00	21.00

Source: Authors' calculations.

BASAT83 = number of satellite channels on basic tiers in 1983–84; *PREM83* = number of available premium channels in 1983–84.

Table B-1 gives sample statistics for the 441 households from the 1992 survey that provided complete information. It also shows the 1983 cable system characteristics for the 278 households in the 1992 survey that were served by a cable system in 1983.

Model Estimates

The results of estimating the multinomial logit model (equation B.15) are shown in table B-2 for four versions of the model. Immediately below each parameter estimate is its t-statistic in parentheses. The top half of table B-2 provides the parameter estimates for the choice to subscribe only to basic

Table B-2. *Summary of Estimated Parameters for Multinomial Logit Model*[a]

Variable	All explanatory variables	Without VCR	Without demographic variables	Naive model
Degrees of freedom	417	419	427	439
Log of the likelihood function	−441.85	−445.31	−463.7218029	−480.55
Basic-only equation				
CONSTANT	−2.75 **	−2.63 **	−0.49	0.22
	(−2.46)	(−2.20)	(−.75)	(1.54)
PRICE	−0.047 ***	−0.040 **	−0.027	
	(−5.99)	(−2.00)	(−0.62)	
BASAT	0.048 **	0.046 **	0.020	
	(2.15)	(2.20)	(0.24)	
OFFAIR	0.072	0.074 ***	0.048 ***	
	(1.37)	(5.21)	(3.50)	
NONDUP	−0.105 **	−0.099 **	−0.099 ***	
	(−2.00)	(−2.53)	(−3.13)	
RURA	−0.240	−0.232	−0.361	
	(−0.74)	(−0.75)	(−0.69)	
LSYSAGE	1.00 ***	1.00 ***	0.43 **	
	(3.37)	(6.39)	(2.18)	
Y	0.0000376	0.0000440		
	(0.54)	(0.72)		
AGE65	1.07 ***	0.960 ***		
	(3.56)	(3.96)		
TIME5	−0.634 **	−0.668 ***		
	(−2.55)	(−4.73)		
FSIZE1	−0.187	−0.272		
	(−0.66)	(−1.22)		
VCR	0.372 ***			
	(8.62)			

cable services. The bottom half provides the estimates for the choice to subscribe to both basic and premium services. The sensitivity of the third choice, no cable subscription, to the economic variables can be inferred from the parameters to these other two choices. The first column of table B-2 presents the model with all of the cable system, geographic, and household variables described earlier.

Tests for Specification

The multinomial logit model must satisfy the requirements of independence of irrelevant alternatives (IIA).[47] This property requires that each al-

47. See Daniel McFadden, "Econometric Models of Probabilistic Choice," in Charles Manski and Daniel McFadden, eds., *Structural Analysis of Discrete Data* (MIT Press, 1981).

Table B-2. *(continued)*

Variable	All explanatory variables	Without VCR	Without demographic variables	Naive model
Basic-plus-premium equation				
CONSTANT	−1.56	−1.14	0.186	−0.097
	(−1.12)	(−0.81)	(0.49)	(0.79)
PREMP	−0.0475 ***	−0.0401 **	−0.0266	
	(−5.99)	(−2.00)	(−0.62)	
BASAT	0.0496 **	0.0448 *	0.0199 ***	
	(2.26)	(1.94)	(7.22)	
PREM	−0.0457	−0.0483	−0.0109	
	(−0.83)	(−0.81)	(−0.10)	
OFFAIR	0.0542	0.0595 **	0.0357	
	(0.84)	(2.04)	(0.24)	
NONDUP	−0.0445	−0.0342	0.00606	
	(0.74)	(−0.75)	(0.34)	
RURA	−1.04 *	−1.05 *	−1.04	
	(−1.67)	(−1.65)	(−0.87)	
LSYSAGE	0.478	0.489 *	−0.0358 ***	
	(1.51)	(1.88)	(−10.94)	
Y	0.000105	0.000118 *		
	(1.31)	(1.69)		
AGE65	0.252	0.0367		
	(0.45)	(0.09)		
TIMES	−0.263	−0.330 **		
	(−0.81)	(−2.13)		
FSIZE1	−0.599	−0.771 **		
	(−1.48)	(−2.09)		
VCR	0.832 **			
	(2.23)			

Source: Authors' calculations.
a. Asymptotic *t*-statistics in parentheses.
* Significantly different from zero at 10 percent confidence interval.
** Significantly different from zero at 5 percent confidence interval.
*** Significantly different from zero at 1 percent confidence interval.

ternative in the multinomial logit model—no cable, basic cable only, and basic plus premium service—is "equally dissimilar." The IIA property would be violated, and the multinomial logit model would consequently be inappropriate if two options were more similar to one another than to the third option. Daniel McFadden developed a test in which the multinomial logit model is nested within a more general model that has an additional parameter whose value is equal to 1.0 if and only if the IIA property holds.[48] We applied this specification test to our model, testing to deter-

48. McFadden, "Econometric Models." See also Jerry Hausman and Daniel McFadden, "Specification Tests for the Multinomial Logit Model," *Econometrica,* vol. 52 (September 1984), pp. 1219–40.

mine if the two cable options are more similar to each other than the third option of no cable. At the 1 percent confidence level we could not reject the hypothesis that the additional parameter is equal to 1.0 and that correspondingly the IIA property holds. We therefore proceeded with the multinomial logit specification.

The specification listed in the first column of table B-2 is not the only one that we examined.[49] The remaining columns present alternative models that restrict some of the parameters of the full specification in the first column. The second column restricts the coefficients on VCR ownership to zero.[50] It is not surprising that we can reject at the 5 percent confidence level the hypothesis that the coefficients on VCR ownership, with large t-statistics in the first column, are zero. We examine in more detail later the relationship between VCR ownership and cable subscription.

Most studies of cable demand do not measure demographic characteristics accurately, if at all (see appendix A). Do demographic characteristics influence demand? We tested the restriction that the parameters on all demographic variables in the multinomial logit model are zero, that is, that the third column of table B-2 is the appropriate model. At any reasonable confidence level, we rejected the hypothesis that all parameter values are zero.[51] In short, household demographics matter. Finally, in column four of table B-2 we examine a naive model that holds that the likelihood of cable subscription is invariant with changes in all the cable system, demographic, and geographic variables used in column one. We resoundingly reject this hypothesis.[52]

Our basic model assumes that households select from among three options: no cable services, basic services, or basic plus premium services. The same decision can, however, be modeled as a dichotomous choice: no cable services or cable services.[53] We estimated this dichotomous logit model, and the results are shown in table B-3. The hypothesis that the parameters of the choice of the basic-only and basic-plus-premium options can be

49. We also examined other cable system, geographic, and demographic variables, but we found the variables in table 3-1 to be the best predictors of household cable choice.

50. We estimated versions of the model with an instrumented VCR-ownership variable, but we cannot reject the hypothesis that the parameter values for cable price and quality variables are unaffected.

51. The chi-square statistic is 44 with 10 degrees of freedom.

52. The chi-square statistic is 77 with 22 degrees of freedom.

53. Much of the empirical literature on demand for cable services is implicitly oriented toward the dichotomous choice framework by not treating demand directly as choice among more than two options.

Table B-3. *Estimated Parameters for Simple Logit Model of Noncable Households*[a]

Variable	Statistic	Variable	Statistic
CONSTANT	−0.147	RURA	0.774 **
	(−0.94)		(2.32)
PRICE	0.0405 *	LSYSAGE	−0.383
	(1.82)		(−1.27)
PREMP	0.0139	Y	−6.40E-05 ***
	(1.22)		(−2.74)
BASAT	−0.0285 *	AGE65	−0.685 *
	(−1.79)		(−1.71)
PREM	0.0983	TIMES	0.494 ***
	(1.47)		(2.75)
OFFAIR	−0.0655	FSIZE1	0.263
	(−1.37)		(0.48)
NONDUP	0.0934	VCR	−0.445 **
	(1.09)		(−2.56)

Source: Authors' calculations.
a. Degrees of freedom, 427. Log of the likelihood function, −467.7040614. Asymptotic *t*-statistics in parentheses.
* Significantly different from zero at 10 percent confidence interval.
** Significantly different from zero at 5 percent confidence interval.
*** Significantly different from zero at 1 percent confidence interval.

restricted to be the same can be rejected at any reasonable confidence level.[54] Consequently, we reverted to the multinomial logit model.

Given the results of these specification tests, our preferred model was the full model presented in the first column of table B-2. All further discussion of results thus refers to the parameters in the first column of this table.

Goodness of Fit

The multinomial logit model implicitly calculates likelihoods that a household, with given demographic and geographic characteristics and facing certain cable system characteristics, will select each of the three options: no cable subscription, subscription to basic services only, and subscription to both basic and premium services. These estimated likelihoods vary with the distribution of household, geographic, and cable characteristics. Table B-4 presents the distribution of the likelihood of demand to each of the three options evaluated at the actual values of the 1992 sample. The mean of the estimated probabilities is nearly the same as the mean of the actual distribution of choices.

54. The chi-square statistic is 52 with 10 degrees of freedom.

Table B-4. *Distribution of Estimated Probabilities of Households Selecting One of the Three Cable Options*

Probability of selecting	Actual value	Estimated mean for 441. households	Standard deviation for 441 households	Minimum estimate for a household	Maximum estimate for a household
No cable	0.317	0.317	0.136	0.067	0.766
Basic only	0.395	0.395	0.147	0.077	0.819
Basic plus premium	0.288	0.288	0.131	0.036	0.703

Source: Authors' calculations.

The estimated probabilities vary substantially, and the predicted values associated with the largest estimated likelihood do not necessarily match actual choices closely. Table B-5 compares the actual household choices with the predicted choices from the full model as well as various restricted versions examined in chapter 3. The full model predicts better than the restricted forms of the model—particularly for choices other than basic only—but it still would not predict the correct one of three choices in more than half of households. Clearly, our model is not capturing all of the information that forms a basis for a household's decision of whether to subscribe to cable television.

Sensitivity of Demand to Cable Service Quality

We delineated our model's implicit estimates of the sensitivity of cable demand to basic service fees in chapter 3. Demand for cable service is also sensitive to premium cable rates. Table B-6 displays the mean probabilities for different cable options for our sample of households under assumptions of a 10 percent increase in premium rates and a 10 percent decrease. At the sample mean, a 10 percent increase in premium rates leads to approximately a 9 percent decrease in the number of households demanding premium services.[55] A 10 percent decrease in premium rates leads to a 10 percent increase in households with a premium subscription. Households would be attracted to premium subscriptions whether they had basic subscriptions or did not subscribe at all. Demand for cable services appears to be slightly more sensitive to premium cable prices than to basic cable prices.

55. Our analysis does not capture multiple premium subscriptions per household.

Table B-5. *Frequency Distributions of Actual and Predicted Cable Choices for the 1992 Sample of Households*

Predicted choice	Full model equation (B.15)	Full model without VCR	Without demographic variables	Naive model
Actual choice: 140 households choose no cable				
No cable	60	59	26	0
Basic only	51	53	78	140
Basic and premium	29	28	36	0
Percentage correct for no cable	43	42	19	0
Actual choice: 174 households choose basic only				
No cable	34	27	13	0
Basic only	102	100	136	174
Basic and premium	38	47	25	0
Percentage correct for basic only	59	57	78	100
Actual choice: 127 households choose basic plus premium				
No cable	25	25	10	0
Basic only	48	57	77	127
Basic and premium	54	45	40	0
Percentage correct for basic and premium	43	35	31	0
Total percentage correct	49	46	46	39
Total percentage incorrect	51	54	54	61

Source: Authors' calculations.

During the period of cable rate deregulation, real premium service rates fell 29 percent, yet the number of premium subscriptions also fell from 46.3 percent of homes passed in 1986 to 45.7 percent in 1992.[56] As a percentage of basic cable subscriptions, premium subscriptions fell more dramatically. Clearly, our cross-sectional model based on 1992 data did not

56. The figure for premium rates is based on the change in average pay rate per month between 1986 and 1992, as reported in Paul Kagan Associates, *Kagan Media Index* (August 31, 1994), p. 3. The figure is adjusted for inflation by the implicit price deflator for personal consumption expenditures.

Table B-6. *Sensitivity of the Sample Mean of the Likelihood of Cable Subscription to Changes in Premium Fees*
Percent

		Choice	
Sample mean	*No cable*	*Basic cable only*	*Basic plus premium cable*
Based on actual system and household characteristics	31.7	39.5	28.8
Based on actual system and household characteristics with 10 percent premium fee increase	32.9	40.9	26.2
Based on actual system and household characteristics with 10 percent premium fee decrease	30.5	37.9	31.6

Source: Authors' calculations.

fully capture changes in demand conditions for premium channels over time. This result is at least consistent with an increasing own-price elasticity of demand over time, quite possibly as the result of new services and technologies that compete with premium cable channels.

The Effect of Quality on Demand for Services

Quality of service, whether measured through the number of basic satellite channels, retransmitted basic broadcast channels, or premium channels, clearly affects demand for cable services. Table B-7 shows the effects of 10 percent changes in the number of basic satellite and broadcast channels. Increasing the number of basic satellite channels by 10 percent increases cable subscription on average by 7 percent. A 10 percent increase in the number of retransmitted broadcast channels yields only a 4 percent increase in the number of cable subscribers. This result suggests that cable operators on average are closer to saturating the demand for broadcast stations than they are for satellite networks, but the result is subject to substantial variation. The coefficient on broadcast channels is not significantly different from zero for either basic or basic plus premium subscription. Also, there is considerable variation among households in the sensitivity of cable subscription to changes in the number of broadcast channels carried by the system.

The likelihood of subscription to premium services appears to be independent of the number of premium services available. There are at least two possible interpretations for this result. First, cable operators may have

Table B-7. *Sensitivity of the Sample Mean of the Likelihood of Cable Subscription to Changes in the Number of Basic Satellite and Broadcast Channels*

	Choice		
Sample mean	*No cable*	*Basic cable only*	*Basic plus premium cable*
Based on actual system and household characteristics	31.7	39.5	28.8
Based on actual system and household characteristics with 10 percent more satellite channels	29.6	40.6	29.8
Based on actual system and household characteristics with 10 percent fewer satellite channels	34.0	38.2	27.8
Based on actual system and household characteristics with 10 percent more off-air channels	30.7	40.3	29.0
Based on actual system and household characteristics with 10 percent fewer off-air channels	32.9	38.6	28.5

Source: Authors' calculations.

reached a point of saturation for premium channels so that additional offerings do not increase subscribership. This interpretation is reinforced by the decline in real premium rates in the late 1980s and the absence of any growth in premium subscribers since 1989.[57] Alternatively, the value of marginal channels may be based on multiple premium subscriptions, which are not captured in the multinomial logit model.

The Effect of Competing Off-the-Air Broadcast Channels

In proceedings on effective competition for cable television before passage of the 1992 Cable Act, the FCC consistently focused on broadcast television as a source of competition for cable operators. Our model revealed that demand for cable services is sensitive to the number of broadcast channels available to households without cable service. Table B-8 shows the effect of changing the number of competing broadcast channels on demand for basic and basic plus premium services in both rural and nonrural areas. As the number of competing channels increases, demand

57. Paul Kagan Associates, *Kagan Media Index* (August 31, 1994), p. 3.

Table B-8. *Sensitivity of the Sample Mean of the Likelihood of Cable Subscription to Changes in the Number of Competing Broadcast Channels*

Percent

Choice	Sample mean based on actual system and household characteristics	Sample mean based on actual system and household characteristics and number of competing broadcast signals								
		2	3	4	5	6	8	10	12	14
Rural										
No cable	39.0	33.4	35.3	37.2	39.1	41.0	44.9	n.a.	n.a.	n.a.
Basic cable only	47.6	53.7	51.7	49.6	47.5	45.4	41.3	n.a.	n.a.	n.a.
Basic plus premium cable	13.4	12.8	13.0	13.2	13.4	13.5	13.7	n.a.	n.a.	n.a.
Nonrural										
No cable	30.1	n.a.	22.0	23.4	24.7	26.1	29.0	32.0	35.1	38.3
Basic cable only	37.6	n.a.	48.0	46.1	44.3	42.5	38.8	35.3	31.8	28.5
Basic plus premium cable	32.3	n.a.	30.0	30.5	31.0	31.4	32.2	32.7	33.0	33.2

Source: Authors' calculations.
n.a. Not available.

Table B-9. *Sensitivity of the Sample Mean of the Likelihood of Cable Subscription to Changes in Household Income*

	Choice		
Sample mean	*No cable*	*Basic cable only*	*Basic plus premium cable*
Based on actual system and household characteristics	31.7	39.5	28.8
Based on actual system and household characteristics with a 10 percent increase in household income	31.3	39.3	29.3
Based on actual system and household characteristics with a 10 percent decrease in household income	32.2	39.6	28.3

Source: Authors' calculations.

for each type of cable service decreases. We found that the competitive effect of broadcast signals continues for all numbers of signals.[58]

Table B-8 also shows a substantial difference in the pattern of demand for cable services between households in rural and nonrural areas. At the sample mean and for any number of competing broadcast signals, households in rural areas are less likely to subscribe to premium channels and more likely not to subscribe to cable at all. This outcome partly reflects differences in sample characteristics; rural households tend to have lower incomes and are less likely to own a VCR. Rural cable systems also average eighteen basic satellite channels; nonrural systems average twenty-four. Even holding these factors constant, rural households were much less likely to subscribe to premium channels than were other households.

The Effect of Household Characteristics

Cable demand is only slightly sensitive to household income. Table B-9 illustrates the effect of 10 percent changes in household income on the demand for cable services. Demand shifts by less than 2 percent. Not surprisingly, demand for premium services is more sensitive to income than is demand for basic cable services.

58. We searched for, but could not find, a natural breaking point beyond which there is no additional competitive effect from broadcast signals.

Table B-10. *Sensitivity of the Sample Mean of the Likelihood of Cable Subscription to Demographic Characteristics*

		Choice	
Characteristic	No cable	Basic cable only	Basic plus premium cable
Age of head of household older than 65	33.1	35.2	31.7
Age of head of household younger than 64	26.6	55.3	18.1
Residence for fewer than five years	28.0	42.0	30.0
Residence for more than five years	34.7	37.5	27.8
One-person household	36.4	46.4	17.3
Multiperson household	30.2	37.2	32.6
VCR owner	28.5	37.4	34.1
Not a VCR owner	39.0	44.1	16.9

Source: Authors' calculations.

The demand for cable services is quite sensitive to other household characteristics. Table B-10 shows the effect on the demand for cable services of the age of the head of household, duration of current residency, size of household, and VCR ownership. Each number in the table represents the actual mean likelihoods for the subsample defined by the description in the stub of the table. For example, in the first entry, among households headed by persons older than sixty-five, the mean likelihood of not subscribing to cable is 33.1 percent. Differences in average likelihoods reflect parametric differences in demand and the distribution of other variables such as system characteristics and household income.

Households headed by individuals younger than age sixty-four are more likely to subscribe to basic cable service but are less likely to subscribe to premium channels. Households that have been at their current residence for less than five years are more likely than others to subscribe to either basic or premium services. Decisions to subscribe to cable are positively influenced by moving. Single-person households are more likely to subscribe to basic service only and less likely to subscribe to premium channels. VCR households are substantially more likely to subscribe to premium channels than are non-VCR households. The importance of household-specific factors in influencing the decision to subscribe to cable television options reinforces our belief that the demand studies for cable that rely on aggregate data for household characteristics are inadequate for making policy judgments about regulation or deregulation.

Compensating Variation

The compensating variation between condition $t = 0$ and $t = 1$ for utility functions from which can be derived logit demand models, such as equation (B.15), can be measured as

$$(\text{B.16}) \qquad D = \lambda^{-1}\left[\ln\left(1 + \sum_{k=1}^{2} (\exp([p^{klt}]\mathbf{b} + [\mathbf{q}k^{ilt}]\mathbf{g}_k \right.\right.$$

$$\left.\left. + [Z^{it},Z^{lt},Y^{it}]\mathbf{d}_k)\right)\right]_{0}^{1}$$

where the square brackets indicate the difference in the expression evaluated at time 1 and time 0, and where λ is the marginal utility of income.[59] We do not observe λ directly in the conditional indirect utility function W. However, from equation (B.9),

$$(\text{B.17}) \qquad -\partial W^*/\partial p^{ilt} \lambda^{-1} = 1 \text{ if } v_j^{*ilt} = V^{*ilt}$$

$$\mathbf{b}\,\lambda^{-1} = 1$$

$$\lambda = -\mathbf{b}$$

Consequently, equation (B.16) can be restated as

$$(\text{B.18}) \qquad D = -\mathbf{b}^{-1}\left[\ln\left(1 + \sum_{k=1}^{2} (\exp([p^{klt}]\mathbf{b} \right.\right.$$

$$\left.\left. + [q^{klt}]\mathbf{g}_k + [Z^{it},Z^{lt},Y^{it}]\mathbf{d}_k)\right)\right]_{0}^{1}$$

1993 Sample of Households

During the early stages of our research, we suspected that our 1992 data set could be improved. For the 1992 Allison Fisher data set, we did not have household-specific expenditures on cable services. Instead, we matched a household's location with the cable system serving that community and cable rate information from Warren Publishing that most nearly matched January 1992. The matching process introduced some possible measure-

---

59. See Small and Rosen, "Applied Welfare Economics with Discrete Choice Models," p. 127.

ment error. Also, the Warren Publishing data were sometimes as much as a year removed from January 1992, another source of measurement error. We considered the choice of premium options as another area of possible data improvement. In the 1992 data set we had information only on the choice of a premium service, not the number or specific selection of premium channels.

To improve the quality of the data, we commissioned a special survey in May 1993 from the same 750 households that were initially surveyed by Allison Fisher. (We used the same sample of households to reduce the collection efforts for geographic information, much of which had already been collected for the households responding to the 1992 survey.) Whereas the 1992 survey was based on a standard form with which the responding households were familiar, our 1993 survey included a special questionnaire on cable expenditures by type of service. We had hoped to obtain from the survey results information on exactly how much households spent on basic cable services, each of several different premium services, and total cable services.

Our initial view of the likelihood and reliability of a household's reporting its cable expenditures in the 1993 survey was perhaps optimistic. Only 488 households surveyed responded to the special questionnaire, much fewer than the 664 that responded to the 1992 survey. Moreover, the responses to many of the questions on the cable expenditure questionnaire were internally inconsistent. For this and other reasons, we found at most 281 complete and consistent responses to the 1993 survey, far fewer than the 441 complete responses to the 1992 survey. Table B-11 presents the sample statistics for these households.

We cannot tell with any certainty how, if at all, the resulting 1993 sample is biased relative to the population of households. It is possible, for example, that households that did not subscribe to cable were less likely to respond to the special questionnaire. It is also possible that households subscribing to premium services had more information to report than other households on the survey form, and consequently were either more likely not to respond or to make inconsistent responses. More than half of the complete responses to the 1993 survey are households subscribing to basic cable service only; in contrast, fewer than 40 percent of households in the 1992 survey made the same choice.

We have little confidence in the service prices reported by households. In communities where more than one household subscribed to the same cable system, we rarely found the same reported basic cable rate, much less

Table B-11. *Sample Statistics for Variables in the Multinomial Logit Model, 1993 Sample*

Variable	Observations	Mean	Standard deviation	Minimum	Maximum
PRICE	281	20.55	4.33	4.95	33.25
PREMP	281	31.10	4.55	15.20	43.70
BASAT	281	23.65	5.97	1.00	38.00
OFFAIR	281	8.65	3.20	0	18.00
PREM	281	5.29	1.53	0	10.00
NONDUP	281	8.18	3.33	0	18.00
RURA	281	0.16	0.36	0	1.00
LSYSAGE	281	2.87	0.44	1.78	3.71
Y	281	3,113.08	2,455.53	416.00	14,583.00
AGE65	281	0.24	0.43	0	1.00
FSIZE1	281	0.25	0.43	0	1.00
VCR	281	0.84	0.36	0	1.00
NOCABLE	281	0.27	0.45	0	1.00
BASIC	281	0.51	0.50	0	1.00
PREMSUB	281	0.22	0.42	0	1.00

Source: Authors' calculations.

rates for other services. In instances where reported rates were implausibly high or low, we deleted the observation from the data set. Ironically, reduction in the measurement error of cable rates in the Warren Publishing data was one of the motivations for the 1993 survey.

We estimated equation (B.15) with the 1993 data set. The results are reported in table B-12. The pattern of estimated parameters is similar to that of the full model from the 1992 sample reported in table B-2. A noticeable difference, however, is the small and insignificant parameter estimate on price. We believe this result may be influenced by measurement error of prices. Nonetheless, we cannot reject the hypothesis that all parameters other than the constant term for the 1993 sample are the same as those for the 1992 sample.

The 1993 survey distinguishes between households that subscribe to one premium channel and households that subscribe to two or more such networks. We estimated a variation of equation (B.15) with four choices: no cable, basic only, basic plus one premium channel, and basic plus more than one premium channel. The parameter estimates were largely insignificant.

The Demand for Premium Services

We can examine demand for individual premium channels based on the 1993 survey. Ideally, the specification of demand for individual premium

Table B-12. *Estimated Parameters for Multinomial Logit Model, 1993 Data Set*

Variable	Statistic	Variable	Statistic
Basic only equation		*Basic plus premium equation*	
CONSTANT	− 3.02 **	CONSTANT	− 3.64 **
	(− 2.13)		(− 1.96)
PRICE	0.000997	*PRICE*	− 0.000997
	(0.03)		(− 0.03)
BASAT	0.0364	*BASAT*	0.0562
	(1.18)		(1.20)
OFFAIR	− 0.00293	*PREM*	− 0.0530
	(− 0.04)		(− 0.503)
NONDUP	− 0.0410	*OFFAIR*	0.0231
	(− 0.60)		(0.23)
RURA	0.229	*NONDUP*	− 0.0649
	(0.46)		(− 0.77)
LSYSAGE	0.777 **	*RURA*	− 0.764
	(2.15)		(− 0.67)
Y	0.0000648	*LSYSAGE*	0.780 *
	(0.76)		(1.77)
AGE65	0.857 *	*Y*	0.0000686
	(1.79)		(0.67)
TIME5	− 0.612 *	*AGE65*	− 0.485
	(− 1.70)		(− 0.52)
FSIZE1	− 0.335	*TIME5*	0.165
	(− 0.89)		(0.33)
VCR	1.16 ***	*FSIZE1*	− 0.203
	(2.79)		(− 0.31)
		VCR	0.563
			(0.72)

Source: Authors' calculations.
a. Degrees of freedom, 257. Log of the likelihood function, − 273.4926476. Asymptotic t-statistics in parentheses.
* Significantly different from zero at 10 percent confidence interval.
** Significantly different from zero at 5 percent confidence interval.
*** Significantly different from zero at 1 percent confidence interval.

channels would include the prices of all premium options as well, and it would be embedded in the broader choices of basic only or no cable. In practice, however, the choice set of premium channels varies across cable systems. In addition, the selection of premium channels is not mutually exclusive, and the number of combinations of outcomes is far greater than our sample size. Rather than incorporate all these combinations in a qualitative response model, we examined more narrowly and separately the demand for each premium channel. We conditioned the sample for the demand model for each premium network to include only cable subscribers facing the choice of that premium network, so that the choice is simply between subscribing to the channel and not subscribing to the channel.

In a manner similar to that implied by expressions (B.2a) — (B.2c), the latent variable associated with the indirect utility function for a cable subscriber not subscribing to an available national premium channel, denoted by subscript k, can be represented as

(B.19a) $\quad v_{1k}^{*ilt} = v_{1k}^{*ilt}(p^{1lt}, q^{1lt}, P^{lt}, Y^{it}, Z^{it}, Z^{lt}, \boldsymbol{\eta}^{it}, \boldsymbol{\eta}^{lt})$,

where k = Home Box Office (HBO), Cinemax, the Movie Channel, Disney, or Showtime. Similarly, the latent variable associated with the indirect utility function for a cable subscriber who subscribes to the national premium channel k can be represented as

(B.19b) $\quad v_{2k}^{*ilt} = v_{2k}^{*ilt}(p^{1lt}, p^{klt}, q^{1lt}, \mathbf{q}^{klt}, P^{lt}, Y^{it}, Z^{it}, Z^{lt}, \boldsymbol{\eta}^{it}, \boldsymbol{\eta}^{lt})$,

where p^{klt} and q^{klt} are the price and quality, respectively, of premium network k at location l at time t. A simple logit variant of this model based on equations (B.19a) and (B.19b) can also be used to examine the decision among cable subscribers to subscribe to premium service k. Let

(B.20) $\qquad v_{ilt} = 1$ if $v_{ilt}^{*} =$ Max (v_{1k}^{*}, v_{2k}^{*})

$\qquad\qquad = 0$ otherwise.

We express v_{ilt}^{*} as in equation (B.7). Further, equations (B.10) and (B.11) hold. We now have, similar to equation (B.15),

(B.21) $\quad$ Prob$(v_{1k}^{ilt} = 1) = (1 + \exp([p^{1lt}]\mathbf{b}_{1k} + [p^{2lt}]\mathbf{b}_{2k}$

$\qquad\qquad\qquad + [\mathbf{q}^{klt}]\mathbf{g}_k + [Z^{it}, Z^{lt}, Y^{it}]\mathbf{d}_k))^{-1}$

$\qquad$ Prob$(v_{2k}^{ilt} = 1) = (\exp([p^{1lt}]\mathbf{b}_{1k} + [p^{2lt}]\mathbf{b}_{2k}$

$\qquad\qquad\qquad + [\mathbf{q}^{klt}]\mathbf{g}_k + [Z^{it}, Z^{lt}, Y^{it}]\mathbf{d}_k)$

$\qquad\qquad\qquad \cdot (1 + \exp(p^{1lt}]\mathbf{b}_{1k} + [q^{2lt}]\mathbf{b}_{2k}$

$\qquad\qquad\qquad + [\mathbf{q}^{klt}]\mathbf{g}_k + [Z^{it}, Z^{lt}, Y^{it}]\mathbf{d}_k))^{-1}$,

where the subscript k refers to the kth premium channel; p^{1lt} is the price of basic service at location l at time t; p^{2lt} is the price of the premium service k at location l at time t; q^{klt} is a vector consisting of the number of off-air signals, the number of basic satellite signals, and the number of premium channels offered on the cable system at location l at time t; and the other variables are as defined for equation (B.15). Table B-13 presents the parameter estimates of the logit model of demand for each of the five premium channels.

Table B-13. *Estimated Parameters of Logit Demand Models for Each Premium Channel, 1993 Data Set*[a]

Variable	Cinemax	Disney	HBO	Showtime	The Movie Channel
Number of cable households with access to premium network	179	190	195	167	119
Number of household subscribers	16	19	43	18	10
Degrees of freedom	170	176	181	154	112
Cases correct	166	176	156	153	106
Log likelihood function	−31.58	−47.51	−91.43	−40.75	−19.33
CONSTANT	7.26	4.23	1.87	5.21	9.84 *
	(1.61)	(1.21)	(0.80)	(1.32)	(1.65)
Price of basic	−0.204 ***	−0.121 **	−0.0581	−0.0924	−0.108
	(−3.02)	(−2.29)	(−1.53)	(−1.60)	(−1.34)
Price of premium channel	−0.491 *	−0.430 **	−0.0607	−0.418 *	−0.582 **
	(−1.81)	(−2.31)	(−0.50)	(−1.84)	(−2.46)
BASAT	0.0968	0.00345	0.0140	0.0327	−0.0305
	(1.08)	(0.058)	(0.37)	(0.42)	(−0.32)
PREM	−0.601409584 *	−0.394	−0.131	−0.308	−0.839
	(−1.72401)	(−1.42)	(−0.84)	(−1.04)	(−1.46)

Table B-13. *(continued)*

Variable	Cinemax	Disney	HBO	Showtime	The Movie Channel
NONDUP	0.0860	0.144	-0.0844	0.111	-0.180
	(0.61)	(1.15)	(-1.05)	(0.89)	(-0.699)
OFFAIR	0.244	-0.0416	0.160 **	0.146	0.022
	(1.57)	(-0.31)	(2.00)	(1.05)	(0.09)
RURA		-1.11	-1.61 **	-0.369	-0.840
		(-0.89)	(-2.12)	(-0.29)	(-0.51)
Y	-0.0000152	0.0000370	0.0000107	0.0000370	0.00015
	(-0.09)	(0.33)	(0.12)	(0.29)	(0.71)
LSYSAGE	-0.897	0.0618	-0.336	-0.679	0.648
	(-1.03)	(0.08)	(-0.73)	(-0.95)	(0.49)
AGE6S	-2.41 *	0.838	-1.70 ***	-2.11 *	-0.14
	(-1.73)	(1.12)	(-2.80)	(-1.68)	(-0.10)
TIME5	1.35 *	-0.118	0.922 **	0.79	-1.40
	(1.74)	(-0.18)	(2.24)	(1.21)	(-1.24)
FSIZE1	0.936	0.0732	0.51	-0.806	0.650
	(1.07)	(0.09)	(1.09)	(-0.89)	(0.57)
VCR	-1.57	1.04	-1.02	-1.11	
	(-1.03)	(0.83)	(-1.55)	(-0.87)	

Source: Authors' calculations.
a. Asymptotic *t*-statistics in parentheses.
* Significantly different from zero at 10 percent confidence interval.
** Significantly different from zero at 5 percent confidence interval.
*** Significantly different from zero at 1 percent confidence interval.

The parameter estimates in Table B-13 generally have the expected signs, but most estimates are not significantly different from zero. With the exception of HBO, each premium channel has fewer than twenty household subscribers in our 1993 sample. With so few observations making distinct choices, a logit model is not likely to have many significant estimated parameters. Moreover, because households often select more than one channel at a bundled rate, a simple logit model of individual premium channel selection, such as equation (B.21), cannot be easily nested within a multinomial logit model that has as a choice the selection of any premium channel, such as in equation (B.15). Consequently, we cannot formally test whether the parameter estimates in table B-13 are consistent with those in table B-2.

Index